Alvah C Bessie
1925

THE IMPERIAL ORGY

BY EDGAR SALTUS

'PETER AT THE MARRIAG

OF HIS FAVORITE DWARF

The Imperial Orgy

An Account of the Tsars from the First to the Last ❧ ❧ ❧ ❧

EDGAR SALTUS

New York ❧ ❧ ❧ ❧

Boni & Liveright

(Incorporated) ❧ ❧ 1920

1453

To
O. S. C.

THE IMPERIAL ORGY

LIST OF ILLUSTRATIONS

THE IMPERIAL ORGY

"Hell bows down before the tsar."

SWINBURNE

TSARS AND TSARITSAS

FROM IVAN TO CATHERINE II

THE IMPERIAL ORGY

I

IVAN THE TERRIBLE

TIMUR and Attila dwarf Ivan but not very much. In the fury with which Attila pounced on civilisation there is the impersonality of a cyclone. Timur was a homicidal maniac with unlimited power and a limitless area in which to be homicidal. Where he passed he left pyramids of human heads and towers made of prisoners mixed with mortar. Where Attila passed he left nothing.

Ivan turned cities into shambles and provinces into cemeteries. A cholera, corpses mounted about him. But death was the least of his gifts. He discovered Siberia. That was for later comers. For his immediate subjects he discovered something acuter. To them he was not cholera, he was providence.

From some he had the epidermis removed, after which they were flayed. Others he carved, a leg or an arm at a time, which he fed to hounds but seeing to it that the amputated were sustained with drink, that their vital organs were protected, seeing to it that they were tended, nursed, upheld, enabled as long as possible to look on at the feast of which their limbs were the courses. Others, tied in sacks, were trampled by maddened horses. But some danced to his piping. Put in cages they were burned alive.

The red quadrilles were invented not by him but by the dancing masters whom history called conquerors and who developed into kings. These beings were divine. They had the right to slay and crucify and they did crucify and slay those that wished to be free and those also that had disrespectful thoughts. To wish to be free was sacrilege. To be disrespectful was contrary to every law. In either case the penalty was death preceded by torture and what could be more reasonable? All men are mortal. To them all a divine providence dispensed the greatest possible variety of ills. Kings who were themselves divine imitated it all they could. It was in this manner that Ivan became a providence to his people.

Born in the early part of the sixteenth century and crowned when a lad, for nearly fifty years his sceptre was an axe. He killed, as hæmatomaniacs do kill, for the joy of it. Before killing he tortured. That also was a joy. It was not only a joy, it was his right. He possessed, in fee-simple, a sovereign monoply of evil.

To-day it seems incredible. There is something that exceeds it. To his quivering people he was a god, a god to be feared as divinity should be, but also to be adored. In life a mythological monster and in death a satyr, he was beloved. That is the incredible. It is also irrefutable. Karamsin, the historian of the early tsars, states it with pride. His statement annalists of the day confirm. When Ivan died, the nation in its entirety, not excepting the children of his victims, put on sackcloth and ashes. The horrors of his reign had fascinated Muscovy to the point of insanity.

In the history of Western Europe there is no parallel for his atrocities, nor is there any for the servility with which they were endured. In considering that abjection one cannot but conjecture that his subjects were insane. Perhaps they were. The acceptance of atrociousness is as insane as its perpetration. None the less and assuming the insanity of all concerned, Ivan had a purpose. That purpose he achieved. He put a seal on Russia, the seal imperial which was blood-red.

Russia then was Cimmerian. Ages earlier, to poets who had not been there, it was a land where gnomes fought for gold with griffons in the dark. The poetry tempted adventure. Triremes entered the Euxine, beyond whose hither coast the gold was rumoured to be. It must have gone, the goblins with it. Instead were whelps of demons that clothed themselves in human skins and who, through gaps of time, vanished utterly. It was forgotten that they had been. They were but brooding. In septentrional fens they lurked, separating and segregating into clans affiliated and yet distinct.

Ultimately, from the White Sea to the Black, a horde descended. They called themselves Slav, a word that means glory. The territory that they occupied was outside of Europe, outside of the world. Unknown, it had no name. It was not until the ninth century that it got one. The Slavs, meanwhile, might have been content to continue to be, had not the scenario of events prevented. Unknown, they were unmolested, consequently they fought among themselves, fought in fights internecine and therefore the fiercer, from which the victors emerged masters and the vanquished slaves. Masters are not necessarily amiable. These also fought and for the very human reason that each wanted to lead.

Equality does not tolerate grades. Precedence being impossible, from the roof of the world they haled a Norse pirate and gave him the *pas*.

The pirate was Rurik. He was chief of a crew of rowers, that is to say, of russi. Russia came then into being and with her a throne that was to become the tallest bit of furniture on earth, a throne so tall that when the last incumbent was tossed from it into Siberia, the trajectory was wider and higher than any that history has beheld. Vespasian, when his hour had come, gestured finely:—"This is death and an emperor should meet it standing." At death's approach, it is said that the last of the Russian emperors fainted.

Rurik was not emperor. He was the turnkey of the enigmatic door that opened on a history that was to be an uninterrupted crime and which, already a sea of blood, mirrored then a record of murders, sacks and massacres; a chronicle of nightmares tangled, obscure but always atrocious, and yet merely preludes, the overture to an empire's gestation or, more exactly, the preliminaries to the construction of the cage in which, bent double, the empire was to live.

From the sea of blood, pictures mount; gleams radiated from Byzantium, ascending cupolas, glittering domes, the torches of civilisation, art and beauty—submerged suddenly by an avalanche of Asiatics shoved over the Urals by the Khan of khans; the conquest of Russia by the Mongols; the lording of her by a despot whom it took years to reach.

More dimly are glimpses of peasants, heavy-witted as cattle, feeding like cattle on straw. Behind them rise the outlines of cities: of Novgorod that styled herself My Lord Novgorod, and of Moscow that from Mongol made Russia Muscovite and where the Rurikovitch lifted themselves into tsars. Additionally, there is a Rembrandt touch that was due to the khans. Sprung from hell they had sunk back there. For souvenir they left night.

Russia then was pitch-black, and not black merely but dumb, a desert of ignorance, a land apart, the pasturage of cattle that a hyena ruled. The cattle had one privilege, one only, but in itself very great, the right to obey. Serfdom, an invention of the operatic Boris Godounov, came later. Designed, very liberally, to prevent economic and military deficits, it turned cattle into fixtures, bound the peasant to the soil.

In the days and particularly the nights of Ivan, cattle were free, at least to die. Apart from that added privilege, they were useful to the upper classes, one of which Ivan composed uniquely. The remaining population was made up of prelates, nobles, vassals, whose lives and possessions were Ivan's absolutely, all in all, in the same manner that Russia was. The realm, his personal property, was a private estate. It lacked a fence. About it he ran a ring of forts. The estate became a park. In that park the modern history of Russia begins. In it germinated the seed of progress, the onward policy and the martyrology of uninterrupted crime.

The potential germ Ivan cultivated. Peter forced it into a fruit rotten before it was ripe. In a marvel of canning, Catherine brandied it. The rottenness remained. But the policy, which persisted, transformed a private park into an empire wider than the moon. It extended Russia from polar auroras to tropic blooms. It led the Bear through the Chinashop to the fangs of Japan. The rottenness, obvious there, threw her into convulsions and the delirium that ensued. Then again night closed on her.

Prior to Ivan there had been night only. It

was he who pronounced the Fiat lux. Day
dawned, a day blood-red which Torquemada
looking on, or rather up, from his scarlet seat at
Satan's left, must have envied, and which Domitian, from his sombrer couch at Pluto's right,
may have regretted. Ivan, more sinister than
either, more fiendish than both, was unexceeded
in horror even by the khans.

During their dominion, Russia, shamming
death, lay prostrate. Ivan raised her, not very
much but still a little and left her on her knees.
For centuries that was her attitude. That she
might maintain it the more devoutly there were
tall gibbets and hot vats. These things insure
fealty. To heighten it, to make it instinctive,
Ivan instilled awe.

In the Golden Horde, when the Khan of
khans had dined, a herald announced that minor
khans could eat. It was very gracious. The
graciousness proceeded from a theory, which
Genghiz Khan made a fact, that there is one sun
—one—above, and one emperor—one—on earth.
The rest of the world was offal. With minor
variations, the Assyrian satraps, the pharaohs,
the Cæsars, preluded Genghiz in that aria. It
caught Ivan's ear, suited his voice. Absolutism
with theocracy for leading motif and Tatar tomtoms for accompaniment was the way he ren-

dered it. The aria had echoes and, the tomtoms aiding, so loud were they that yesterday, or the day before, you could have heard them. Through the centuries they reverberated from the first tsar to the last.

Ivan who had taken everything else, took the tomtoms and with them the tomtom players, the trained musicians of the Golden Horde who, in Slavonic, became opritchniki which, being translated, means assassins. At a gesture from Ivan, they cut your head off. Convenient for him, they were quite as convenient for his successors. In descending the centuries their name changed, but not their functions. Yesterday or the day before, they were known as the red guards. Instituted by the first tsar, they eliminated the last. They were certainly very serviceable.

The Descartian *Cogito ergo sum* had not then been formulated. Before it could be, Ivan reversed it. Cogitate and you no longer were. The aria with its tomtom accompaniments regulated not only actions but thoughts. To cogitate was not permitted. Even if it had been, no one dreamed of such a thing. Apart from that, restrictions were few. Obedience only was exacted and everything else forbidden. These measures, eminently considerate, were equally benevolent. Personal notions were sacrilegious and sacrilege, as everybody knows, is punishable not in this world merely, but in the next. Tortured here while you lived, hereafter you were tortured forever.

A very beautiful idea, it had perhaps its defects. It put a premium on imbecility. On the other hand, it created awe. Imbecility is sufficiently common. Awe is more rare. Without it absolutism could not have endured. Yet such are the abysses of human stupidity that wretches whom Ivan was torturing shrieked in their agony, "God save the tsar!"

At tsaral command, millions have vacated the planet. Why? They did not know. They omitted even to ask. Batushka—the Little Father— had so ordered. That sufficed. These people were not very intelligent. Perhaps Ivan was not either.

Karamsin says that he was intelligent. He says also that he was best read man in the realm. That may be true and mean nothing. Barring the Bible and a few histories quite as reliable, there was nothing to read. Ivan read the Bible. The hyena was devout. Religion led him from massacres to mass and back again.

Bluebeard and Caracalla combined, he had seven wives of whom he only killed three. He

tickled a child. The child laughed. He ran
a knife down its throat. A boiar, not seeing him
approach, omitted to grovel. To improve his
sight his legs were broken. Another noble—
But these are minor matters. Generally, the
lackeys of history ignore them. Perhaps they
were due to nervousness. Ivan was born in a
storm which, it may be, predisposes to neurosis.
But also he was born with a sceptre in his mouth.
He was fourteen before he knew how to use it.
At that age, a boiar displeased him. He had
him thrown to the wolves, eaten alive. He was
training then for the throne of Moscow.

In recent years, Moscow was a manufactur-
ing town. Its specialty was silk. In Ivan's
day its specialty was death. In the nineteenth
century, there were high hats, yellow gloves,
women's laughter, the tinkle of the balalaika and
gypsies singing in the streets. In the sixteenth
century, Moscow was dumb. Belfries tolled,
the tocsin sounded. Apart from that there was
silence.

From afar it enchanted. It seemed a city of
sylphs in a land of chimeras. Nearer, it frightened. From afar it projected the glitter of
glass, the sheen of enamel, the glow of mother-
of-pearl, a crystallisation of spangles, ochre,
azure, pink. Fairylike from afar, within was

a conjury of constructions without a name and without example. The architecture was not Tatar, it was not Lower Empire, it was not Gothic. The renaissance had not come there. Greece was absent. Neither oriental or classic, it was tsaral. Around it circled rampants, white and pale rose. Without was Moscow, Russia's Mekka. Within was the Kreml, Moscow's heart.

Ivan was the ideal tyrant. The Kreml was a tyrant's ideal, a city of assassins that looked on a city of victims. Fortress, abattoir, seraglio, acropolis and necropolis in one, for a heart it was infernal.

Ivan was born there, lived there, died there, haunts it still. It was not his work, it was his portrait. With curious foresight it was built by Ivan's grandfather in Ivan's image. The architects were Italian. There were Italian architects everywhere. Nowhere, in no place, at any time, has Italian art created anything in any way similar. Like Ivan it was and remained unique. A charnel house may be grandiose, it cannot be sublime. The Kreml never allured. It did better. It alarmed. At the time, Moscow was the frontier of Europe, a barrier against the East. The Kreml menaced both. In its

IVAN THE TERRIBLE

turrets spectres watched, watch still perhaps.
Like Ivan, it was inhuman.

Without the Kreml, at a turning to the left, is
the Red Square.   In the square is the Church
of Vassili Blagennoi.   The name of the architect is forgotten, but not his fate.   To prevent
him from elsewhere erecting a duplicate, Ivan
tore his eyes out.

To-day it suggests a corner of some universe
other than ours.   But the immediate impression
is one of emancipation.   You feel that the architect was freed from the pale camisoles of what
is correct.   Critics have called him mad.   Perhaps he was.   It is only the mad who are delivered from the commonplace.

Here the deliverance is expressed in a solidi-
fied mirage that resembles a dragon and a peacock topped by flowers on fire, by painted icicles,
by strawberries gigantic and glowing, by roses
and rainbows that bewilder, delight, dismay.
The effect, vividly abnormal, is that of an hallu-
cination.   It is a House of God perhaps, but of
God as men may have known Him in Atlantis,
when faith was nearer to nature than the divine.
Primarily an evocation, it remains a marvel.
Ivan's treatment of the architect has therefore
an excuse, or at least Gautier found one for

him:—"In matters of art, ferocity is preferable · to indifference."

Behind the ferocity is a story that may be untrue but which Karamsin recites. During the siege of Kasan, Tatar sorcerers stood on the walls and with lifted robes vomited spells and insults at Ivan who, Cross in hand, outfaced them. In commemoration of the strategy, and of the victory that ensued, the Church of Vassili the Beatified was erected.

Ivan took Kasan from the Tatars as Ferdinand took Granada from the Moors. That recovery enthralled Castille. The recovery of Kasan enraptured Muscovy. It threw back the Golden Horde. It started the débâcle of the khans. After Kasan, Astrakhan and, with the latter, the Caspian.

These feats are notable. So, too, at the time, was Ivan. He was devout. He was brave. He was handsome. Terrible he was also, but only on the field. Presently his character changed, his appearance altered. Where the Christian had been came the saurian. From handsome he grew hideous. A hyena replaced the hero.

Perhaps a man's courage is in proportion to his humanity. Probably if the latter diminishes so does the former. It may be that psychological variations alter the lines of the face. As a lad, Nero was charming. The epileptically obscene changed him into a cringing beast. That and other influences affected Ivan. Bestial and remorseless at home, to foreign insults he bowed. He did worse, if worse can be.

There was Kasan. He offered to return it. There was Livonia. He gave it back. Livonia was the gate to Europe. Muscovy had fought for it with the Poles, with the Swedes, with the Livonians themselves. Muscovy had won it. Ivan owned it. It was his, with an insult for crown.

He had asked the Polish king for his sister in marriage. The answer he received was a white mare tricked out like a woman. The envoi was the king's expression of his supreme contempt. Ivan swallowed it. Subsequently, with a relatively innumerable army, with a relatively inexhaustible treasure, he surrendered Livonia, not at the point of the sword, but with a scratch of the pen. The bloodiest of sovereigns, who killed an elephant because it did not kneel at his bidding, had grown afraid of a man.

The result is curious. Ivan had seven wives whom he successively ignored, repudiated or killed. By the seventh he had a son, Dmitri, who lives in drama to-day. By the third he had a son, Fedor, who has survived in an opera. By the first there had been born to him the tsarevitch, a lad that he was training in crime and debauchery to reign when he had gone.

After the surrender of Livonia, the tsarevitch asked leave to go and fight the Poles. The request was innocently made; that is, if anything could be innocent in a hyena's whelp. But Ivan, construing the request as a criticism, raised a cudgel and struck him dead. Then, crocodilianly, the hyena wept.

Ivan exceeded Torquemada. He exceeded Tartuffe. Without any intention to abdicate, he announced that he would. It may be doubted that the martyrs loved their Roman butchers or that the Cæsars were affectioned by the saints. But Muscovy, to whom servility was a religion and, psychologically, a very interesting religion, beat her battered head against the throne. With tears and lifted hands she prayed that he would deign to continue to rule. To him, to rule was to kill and justified by the national genuflections, murder became not merely a joy but a duty, one that he so punctiliously fulfilled that, when he died, the desolation experienced was curious and even biblical.

Historically the desolation was profound, yet, unless any present conjecture is hopeless, it must have been less pronounced than the desolation which Ivan himself effected. In spite of his ultimate attitude to Poland, previously he had been terrific.

Poland at the time, predominant in the north, had for emblem the sun. Other tsars attended to that. They put it out. Ivan attended to Novgorod who had been stretching a hand to its rays. The attention involved, first the destruction of the surrounding country. For years it was bare. Famine stalked there and on the heels of famine, plague. Already Ivan had attended to the inhabitants.

Every day for a month, thousands were dispatched. Some were ordered to scaffolds, to cauldrons, to the river, where they were thrown wholesale. Some were hacked to pieces. Others were first hacked and then boiled. In the river, children were tied to their mothers. Guards, armed with pikes rowed among them, shoved them down. The guards and executioners wearied; Ivan never.

Occasionally he prayed. This was his prayer: "Remember, Lord, the souls of Thy servants, inhabitants of this town, whose names Thou knowest."

Incidentally he kept tally. One of the lists gives three thousand four hundred and seventy "whose names Thou knowest." On other lists, names that he had learned are itemised "with his wife," "with his wife and children," "with his sons and daughters."

The prayers at an end, the lists completed and filed, Ivan returned to Moscow where, in the Red Square, at the east wall of the Kreml, other traitors "whose names Thou knowest" waited.

Here were more cauldrons, more gibbets; saws that cut you in two; pincers that pulled your tongue out; machines that slipped you, like an eel, from your skin. Then as, leisurely, the first tortures began, Ivan, foaming like a horse, called at the tortured:—

"I am your god!"

Very consoling and equally true. To a people dumb and driven, he was a god, jealous perhaps, perhaps also severe, but so wholly divine that after the Novgorod ceremonies, ambassadors who passed that way found the Volga dammed by the corpses that the god had left.

For these envoys other things were in store, the surprise of discovering a new realm, a land that stretched between Europe and Asia, a monarchy whose sovereign was more formidable than the khans. It amazed them, as the unimagined always does amaze. But a detail surprised. In the faraway burgs and keeps from which they had come, they were clearly entitled to whatever was not taken away from them. In Russia, matters were ordered differently. There the ruler, after taking everything else, put the iron hand of absolutism on whatever his subjects possessed. Privileges and property, all were his, in fee-simple. Their right to breathe was subject to the caprice of a despot who had taken septentrional sables and bicephalous eagles for device and who called himself tsar.

The sables were indigenous, the eagles Byzantine, but the title tsar, a word that means power, originated in Assyria where it became the terminology of kings, notably of Nabonassar, Nebuchadnezzar, Belshazzar. Muscovy, finding the title in the Slavonian translation of the Bible, gave it to the khans. It was from them that Ivan took it. Antecedent rulers had been grand princes, grand-dukes. In assuming the higher title, Ivan glorified the realm.

In the Kreml, where he held court, it would have been interesting to have seen him. On a throne of gold, that was set with two thousand diamonds—a present from a brother reptile, the Shah—a diadem on his hideous head, in one bloody hand he held the orb, symbol of sovereignty; in the other, the sceptre, symbol of power.

Horsey, an English tourist, who visited him
and who was perhaps imaginative, says that the
sceptre, three feet long, was a whale's tooth
crusted with jewels, and that the robe he wore
was so laden with other jewels that he could not
move.

In that regalia, Ivan, hyena though he were,
must have resembled Arpocrates, god of silence.
About him, in kaftans of white satin, boiars
stood, armed with silver hatchets. They did not
speak. No one spoke. There was not a sound,
not a whisper, not a movement. One would have
thought the court bewitched. In the witchery
of it, in that silence, on that throne, Ivan presented the spectacle—by no means commonplace
—of absolute might. Presently he gestured, the
court awoke and ambassadors and tourists approached the monster, who already divine, had
taken on other aspects of divinity.

After the manner of Tlaloc, the lizard-faced
god of the Aztecs, he made the rain and the fine
weather. Those about him had nothing whatever, and very naturally since he had all. Consequently, on state occasions, he rained sunshine
on them. Guards, nobles, the rest of the court,
were given silks, satin, velvet, gems. The function at an end, the lizard-hyena saw to it that
garments and jewels were returned.

That custom, which he originated, was afterward abrogated, but the theory of it, the theory
that from the tsar everything emanated, that he
alone was, that no one else is anybody, persisted
and so sovereignly that patriotism became
treason.

Treason at this time was not in the code, it
was in the index. Patriotism was fealty and
fealty religion. To the Russian, in his Greek
Church, the tsar, the nation and the Almighty
were entities barely differentiable. That idea,
lunatic certainly, but an article of faith, endured
and in enduring inspired, as it was intended to
inspire, such awe that, until within relatively
recent years, Russians got from their convey-
ances and threw themselves in the mud, in the
snow, before a tsar as he passed.

Through a beautiful subversion of this idea,
prelates in announcing Ivan's death, proclaimed
that he had become an angel. At the death-
notice Muscovy really grieved. That in itself
partakes of the marvellous. What perhaps is
more marvellous still is that with the grief astonishment mingled. An angel! It was unac-
countable and not at all because of his fiendishness but because of local servility. An angel!
Could he not have done better? Without effort

it had been assumed that when he deigned to die he would be translated to the zenith ineffable.

Balzac said that it is not possible to conceive of an ugly angel.   Perhaps he forgot Ivan who, just prior to his assumption, contrived to sully even the Kreml.   Between those lines there is drama.   Karamsin supplied the details.   From them Alexis Tolstoi wrote a play:—*The Death of Ivan the Terrible.*

The mise en scène is a horrible room in the palace of horrors.   In that vomitory of crime, Ivan, stretched on a bed of zibelines, was momentarily alone.   Boris Godounov, a wolfman, had just left him.

Without, guarded by keepers, were men in peaked bonnets and the long, starred robes of Babylon.

It was adjacently that Ivan lay, but not quite alone.   Death that tore tiaras from popes and sceptres from kings, reducing them all to the great proletariat of eternity, was there also. The men in starred robes had foretold it.   Unknown to them, unknown, too, to Ivan, the wolfman had invited it.

A little before, from the red stairway of the red palace, Ivan had seen a comet.   Was it a presage of his passing, he wondered?   That he might know, he had summoned magicians, as-

sembled astrologers, promising that if they lied
he would kill them.

At the moment, to minister to Ivan, timidly,
atiptoe, the wife of his son Fedor entered and
fled aghast at his instant and monstrous lubric-
ity.

Ivan laughed. Death? He had shamed it
from him. Laughing still, he clapped. A
page appeared. Ivan ordered. The soothsayers and their guards filed in.

Ivan, indicating the wizards, told the guards
to take them out, take them away and burn them
alive. They had lied. They had said he was
to die that day. Make a bonfire of them!

Ivan turned, turned again. "Wait! The day
is not done. Hold them until night. Then,
the stake!

"Here!" he called at approaching pages.
"Lead me to my treasure-hall."

That hall was floored with agate, roofed with
gold. In it, jewels were heaped. There were
bags of emeralds, bags of rubies, bags of pearls.
There were crowns there, the crown of Muscovy,
the crown of Kasan, the crown of Kiptchak, the
crown of Siberia, the crown of Astrakhan,
crowns on crowns, diamonds on gold, dust on
blood. There were great silver bins piled one
on top of the other, each replete with coin, with

the sack of cities, with the spoil of provinces, with the riches of realms, with spectres, with tears.

With widening eyes, the miser-satyr stared. The hall had faded, the crowns had vanished, the glare had gone. There was nothing, blood only and mists of murdered men.

He wavered, staggered, fell. From out the mist death had leaped.

Ivan the Angel was winging his way on high.

A table remained. It was set. On it were chalices of power, flagons of grandeur, cups of mud and blood. The wine was there, the feast prepared. The imperial orgy had begun.

II

DMITRI THE SORCERER

GREECE had many shrines. There was one to every divinity. There was one to the unknown god. In Rome there were altars to every sin, except the sins unknown. Unknown sins were unimaginable. Two, that have become known since then, are indescribable. To-day, in words masked to the teeth, one is called cloacism; the other, masochism. Invented by the Tatars for the relaxation of batrachians and ghouls, afterward they were forgotten until, in Flanders and Champagne, they were revived by the Huns.

Ivan adopted them, took to them naturally, took to religion also. Ferocious felons are often devout. In the cathedrals of contemporaneous Spain, highwaymen sharpen their daggers while saying their prayers. From saurian abysses Ivan passed to the cloister. There he prostrated himself, protested his abasement, after which he returned to it.

During one of his religious crises, a son,

Fedor, was conceived. He had another son, the lad whom he killed, and still another, Dmitri who was also killed, killed twice, killed three times, killed oftener perhaps, but who, in each instance, came to life again.

Russian history is packed with drama. In point of time, in point, too, of surprise, the Dmitri drama leads. Schiller attempted it, Goethe considered it, Soumarokov wrote it. It will be told in a moment. The story of Fedor comes first. Brief and unusual, it is like the tale of the Persian king who, invisible to his subjects, occupied himself with beautiful things.

Before Ivan became an angel, he instituted a pentarchy, a council of five—five boiars—nominally a ministry of affairs domestic and foreign, but whose actual ministry was limited to variations on the Byzantine formula:—"May I speak and live?" Among the five was Boris Godounov, whose sister Fedor had married. Ivan gone, the pentarchy led Fedor to the feast, seated him there, set the chalices before him.

A dilettante in delicate emotions, the food was too rich, the wine too strong. Beyond were Persian tapestries. Abandoning the orgy to Boris, he retired behind them and thereafter occupied himself in going to mass and avoiding his wife.

The charm of missals—missals that pictured

the twelve perils of hell—the ecstasy apprehensible in devotion, the harmony of grave hymns, the glow of ikons, these things appealed to him in ways which blood and mud never could. With fine levity, history has called him chaste. At least he was neither sensual nor drunken, abstentions very remarkable in those days and particularly in a son of Ivan. Fedor resembled his father as a fawn resembles a boa-constrictor. The table with its high festoons failed to detain him. But, an artist, he embellished Moscow. He gave it an avenue on which, in lieu of the pine isbas of Ivan's day, there were palaces, uncomfortable, unsanitary, but of stone, and more churches—already there were five hundred—and among them one in particular, a little gem, that held just seven souls.

On the palace walls he hung paintings that displayed the leading chapters of Russian history, the main events of the Bible. In the middle rotunda, from which a red stairway led, he put mosaics of saints and seraphs and, behind a screen of jewels, the Madonna. Above, in the centre of the arched roof, he added a sculptured lion holding in its teeth a twisted serpent from which the tsaral eagles swung. Beneath was the throne which he supplemented with the four monsters of the Apocalypse. These were of gold, the throne was gold, the walls were gold and about them he put gold and silver vases, some in the form of licornes and stags, others in the form of swans and peacocks and all so massive that, Karamsin says, it took a dozen men to move one of them.

These decorations effected, Fedor became a Persian king. It fatigued him to rule. From despotism he shrank. No tsar has been more the artist and less the autocrat than he. But no tsar has been artist at all—except in the divine business of ordering people off the earth. In that, each of the litter was hors concours. Fedor, with no criminal tendencies, with no orgiac tastes, effaced himself, abandoning Muscovy to a wolf.

Beauvois de Chauvincourt wrote learnedly on lycanthropy, concerning which it used to be heretical to disbelieve. Boris Godounov presented a prefectly defined case. A magnificent brute, Tatar on the distaff side, he looked the wolf, lived the wolf and made others die of that wolfishness. In the orgy that Ivan initiated, raveningly he had assisted. Very close to Ivan and always edging closer, finally he closed in on him. Ivan's abrupt ascension was caused by a poisoned brew which the wolf cooked and served him. The brew brought him close to the

BORIS GODUNOV

throne, to which he got closer, still closer, until he hugged it.

To-day, in operatic circles, his basso howl resounds. Moussorgski did reasonably well by him, though less happily perhaps than Glinka did with Mikhail Romanov, the insignificant insect around whom he composed *A Life for the Tsar*. One may regret that instead of that insect he did not take Fedor. The regret is idle. It was Fedor's destiny to live less in scores than in sanctity, a sancity, parenthetically, which Dmitri, his thoroughly demoniac brother, exceeded.

Dmitri, then a boy of seven, was a little savage, a trifle malformed. One of his arms was longer than the other. With his mother, he lived obscurely and afar at Ouglitch where he tortured kittens and puppies and made models in snow of the chief boiars whose heads he chopped off. The story of these traits, very promising, thoroughly Ivanesque, was probably invented. But Fedor was childless; also he was frail. The little savage was next in line. Boris licked his chops at both. One at a time.

Presently the little savage was murdered, or so it was reported. In those days murder was common and not at all criminal. But a tsarevitch was holy. His assassination was sacrilege. Immediately the obituary was corrected.

Dmitri had not been murdered. He had killed himself, accidentally, while at play, during which, knife in hand, he had a fit of epilepsy and the knife had cut his throat. The story may not be true, but at any rate he was dead, though how he died witnesses differed. That was very injudicious of them. The official version must prevail. Dmitri's mother was sent to a convent, other witnesses to their graves. Ouglitch was razed, the inhabitants exterminated. During the massacre, a bell tolled. What business had it to do that? Karamsin says that Boris exiled it, shipped it to Siberia. Excellent measure.

Dmitri then was thoroughly dead. Years later to make him deader, if that were possible, he was beatified and made a saint. In the Greek Church, to which orthodox Russia adhered, canonisation was less arduous than at Rome. The proponent's tomb was opened. If the body had not decomposed that miracle attested his sanctity. But a bone is part of the body; at a pinch, so, too, is a lock of hair. Given but these and the miracle subsisted. They sufficed for the young savage. Moreover, when his tomb was opened, a perfume, rarely delicious, issued from it. That in itself was enough, yet there was more. His remains, a bone and a hank of hair worked the usual wonders, effected the usual cures. In the same measure that Dmitri's death was beyond doubt, so also was his sanctity.

All this was years later. Fedor meanwhile had joined his angelic father. Boris remained. His sister blessed him; the boiars knelt to him. A wolf was tsar.

In his lair was a daughter, Xenia. Her eyebrows met, a mark of beauty then greatly admired and which when lacking was produced with a crayon. Baer, a Lutheran clergyman who was in Moscow at the time and who left a little bloody history of it, said that she seemed moulded in cream and spoke more elegantly than a book.

The rumour of these charms allured the Prince of Denmark to Moscow, where, although he was a foreigner, consequently a heretic and hated as such, Boris so feasted him that he died. It was said that he had been poisoned. Probably that was untrue, but thereafter other princes fought shy of this beauty for whom fate had in store a rôle which, on another stage, Louise de la Vallière immortalised.

Incidentally there were tortures, decapitations, butcheries, wars and sacks. Boris Godounov was becoming very terrible. There was a famine more terrible still, during which human flesh hung in the markets and a mother was seen eating her child.

With these harmonies for overture, the curtains parted on one of the great dramas of Russian history. At the court of Sigismond, king of Poland, abruptly, like a knight in a ballad, the dead Dmitri appeared. Sardou never did better.

Whether it were the real Dmitri, whether it were an impostor, or, as was afterward said, a sorcerer that then occupied the stage, no one now can say and, it may be that, save the chief actors, no one then could. The tale that was told was that relatives at Ouglitch, fearful of Boris and his wolfishness, had substituted a dead boy for the tsarevitch who was then hidden in a monastery which, years later, he abandoned and afterward joined the Cossacks.

The Cossacks, literally the Fighters, were hordes on horseback that had republics that were armies, but no chiefs, except in war, when they elected a despot and called him hetman. Among the cavalry republics was that of the Cossacks of the Don. Dmitri joined them and declared his rank, exhibiting, to prove it, various tokens; in particular, a cross of diamonds.

Diamonds then were not the articles of commerce that they have since become. Inhibited to the vulgar, they were reserved to the elect. Generally, there were laws on the subject: what is more potent, there were terrors. To anyone not born to the purple, the possession of a diamond was malefic. The evil repute of that hill of light, the Koh-i-nor, has no other origin. A belief in this malignancy, common among the simple to-day, was potent then. Moreover the pretender, young, virile, ugly—ugly with that ugliness that attracts—had an air sovereign and compelling. He looked the king. In addition to the cross, his appearance may have been confirmatory. In any event it served as passport to the court of Sigismond, who, perhaps, had issued the passport himself. That is possible. It may be that the claimant was really prince, but with the bend sinister, a natural son of this king who, for reasons of his own, wanted him on the throne of Russia.

Russians and Poles were like first cousins that loathe each other. Mutually antipathetic, they came of the same stock. But while the Poles, in their relative freedom, had developed the Slavic grace and gallantry, the Russians, under the Tatars, had degenerated into ignorant and superstitious brutes. Bathory, the antecedent king of Poland, had proposed to reunite the two nations. The proposition, advanced to Fedor, was rejected by Boris, fearful for his own regency and the domination which the superior civilisation might exert.

Sigismond, in seconding Dmitri, may have had the same idea. But that is conjectural, as is almost everything else concerning Dmitri, except that he was a demon and, what is far rarer, a man. He may have been Sigismond's son. He may have been Ivan's. He may have been neither. Concerning his origin there are texts by the ton, opinions all you like, but a certainty never, unless a mother's recognition may be so regarded. The mother of Dmitri Redux did recognise him as her son, or pretended to, and must have pretended, if pretend she did, because she was terrorised into it. Between those horns of the duenna, the reader may choose. The rest is fairy-tale, very bloody, equally dramatic, with a coup de théâtre for finale.

At Sigismond's court, Dmitri Redivivus encountered Iouri Mniszech, lord palatin of Sendomir, a great noble as greatly in debt, who also had a daughter, Maryna, another beauty, prima donna in the lyric drama that ensued. At first sight the two young people fell in love. Life became fair as a dream. The impoverished father sanctioned the engagement, the subtle king offered an army. Both had the throne in view:

Sigismond perhaps for himself, Mniszech certainly for his daughter. But while it does not appear that the king made any conditions, the father demanded sacks of the Kreml gold. To get the girl, Dmitri had to get the gold and to get the gold he had first to get the throne. It was the old Hesperidian story, told backward, told in Slav.

The encounterable difficulties were formidable. Boris had an army to maintain him. But here, as in every fairy-tale, the unbelievable enters. Muscovy, enthralled by the story of the resurrection of her lawful lord and weary of a werewolf's teeth, rose to Dmitri. The troops refused to fight against Ivan's son and heir. Very sensibly, too. At Dmitri's heels were long vistas of Poles and Cossacks; the former brilliant, glittering, yet frightful with the wings of great vultures which they wore on their helmets; the latter soberly and sombrely fierce.

Among the Muscovite troops, Boris, by way of counter-irritant, circulated a quadrille of monks who were, or who claimed to be, superiors of the monastery where the pretender had been. Violently they denounced him as an impious impostor, a youth of base origin whom again and again they had punished and for what? For sorcery!

The accusation, which afterward was shudderingly recalled, Dmitri traversed. He trapped the monks, put them to the question. On the peaks of torture three of them died. The fourth recanted. Dragged before Dmitri he collapsed, but he gasped:—"Behold the tsar!" In an effort to get him to his feet, those that stood about kicked him. He was dead.

The testimony lacked conclusiveness. To confirm it, something else was required. Dmitri's mother was in a convent. He invited her to join him. They met in a tent, very sumptuous, it is said, that had been erected for the purpose at the outskirts of Moscow. Within the tent, concealed from all, for a few moments they remained. Then, issuing from it, they embraced; the tsaritsa publicly acknowledging Dmitri as her son. Afterward, she was said to have said that, while in the tent, Dmitri threatened to kill her if she refused. That may or may not be true. But, at the time, who could doubt that he were tsar?

No one perhaps, not even Boris, particularly not Boris. The loupgarou may not have known the truth about Dmitri, but he knew it then about himself. In Beauvois de Chauvincourt's learned and very reasonable work on lycanthropy, it is stated that when a werewolf is cornered and cannot escape, he kills himself. Boris Godounov drank poison and just in time. Through the holy gate of holy Moscow, Dmitri was riding. He rode a white charger whose legs and tail had been dyed scarlet, a picturesque conceit intended to suggest that the horse had waded through blood.

At the entrance, dignitaries in gala dress tendered him a gold plate on which were bread and salt, the symbols of submission. Dmitri flung himself from that horse—the detail is typical—and strode—another typical detail—into the palace where, perhaps after an old manner of paying old debts, he made the fascinating Xenia his. The coronation followed and for a while this lad, he was only twenty-one, lived in state with a tsarevna for mistress.

In fairyland, kings and queens never appear without their crown and to Dmitri, the Kreml, vomitory of crime though it were, must have been fairyland then. Whether prince or impostor, his life had been rude. Hunger had been his bedfellow, peril his drink and suddenly, through one of the prodigious shuffles of fate, he was tossed from nowhere into everything.

Above him swung a gold bicephalous bird. Beneath the eagle was a panoply of canary brocade festooned with pearls that silver griffons upheld. Beneath the panoply, on a throne of gold, in a golden robe, he sat. About him were prelates in purple; princes in ermine. On his head was the crown; in his hand the sceptre. But at his feet, in the attitude of a slave, a man, old, fat, dressed and bejewelled as now only maharajahs are, held, with venomous and greedy fingers, the imperial sword.

That man, that slave, whom Dmitri had first disgraced and then raised to the position of valet, was Vassili Chouiski. Watch him! He is the villain in this drama of which all that has gone before is prelude.

Years earlier, in the remote obscurity in which the savage young tsarevitch lived, Vassili's had been the arm chosen by Boris to eliminate him. A Rurikovitch and as such with claims of his own to the throne, he had done the work, not for Boris, but for himself, a design which Boris thwarted. Since then he had bided and brooded and plotted and for what? At the very moment when he might have called Muscovy his, the dead young savage had revived, not merely to thwart him again but to disgrace him. Publicly, in the Red Square, Dmitri had had him knouted, as a preliminary to chopping his head off. Then, just when the axe was raised, Dmitri had laughed and pardoned, yet only to send him to Siberia and, as the cart was starting, had laughed anew, pardoned once more and made him his valet. Such vengeance might have envenomed a saint. Vassili was not a saint. A wretched, greedy old man, he bided and plotted.

With the careless temerity of youth, Dmitri abetted him. At the very beginning, in flinging himself from the crimson-legged charger and in striding into the palace, he affronted Moscow. A prince of Muscovy never strode. When he deigned to walk, though it were from one room to another, boiars supported him. When he rode, they lifted him up, held him in the saddle, lifted him down, treating him always like an idol. Dmitri was grand-duke and tsar, but primarily a man. He derided old customs and with them the abysmal Muscovite ignorance, which, like all else that was orthodox, Russia revered.

Former grand dukes amused themselves with bear fights which they enjoyed from a balcony. A fight was arranged for Dmitri. He abandoned the balcony and killed the bear. It was a tsar's privilege to kill his subjects. But a bear, no. Moscow drew the line at that.

A yet graver affront was Dmitri's entourage. All Poles, they were all pagans, as all foreign-

ers were. Other nations professed other creeds.
That was their damnation. Russia alone was
holy. Throughout the universe her lord was
the one Christian king, and all other kings his
slaves. But was Dmitri a Christian? Was
he even Muscovite? He allowed the Polish
hussars to enter the Church of the Mother of
God with clanking swords and to squat there,
leaning against the sacred ikons, to which he
never bowed. His priests, it was said, were
papists. But when it was said also that he was
to marry a heretic, it was suspected that he could
not be a Russian at all, rather, as Vassili Chouiski insinuated, a hireling employed by Sigismond to deliver Muscovy to the Polish king.

As novelists express it, the ground was prepared.

Into the gloom of the Kreml, Xenia meanwhile was fading. From a delight, she had become an ennui; from a vision, a shadow. Deeper
into the gloom she passed. A convent opened
and swallowed her. Dimitri nodded good-riddance. He, too, was preparing. Maryna was
en route.

Already the treasure-chests had been opened.
The sacks of gold were paid. Then, at last,
came the bride. But to Moscow, how indecently!

In a chariot drawn by eight horses that were tricked out and painted to resemble tigers, she appeared, dressed after the manner of Marie de Medici, with a ruff two feet in diameter, a ballooning skirt, a waist that would fit in a garter, her hair done high and, like her waist, exposed.

In Muscovy, the hair of a Christian woman was concealed by a headgear. Always her gown was girdled above the breast. Never had Moscow seen such an exhibition. The old orthodox city was not placated by the presence of the girl's father, nor by the presence of a chaperon, mistress of the robes. For behind the heretics, trooped a retinue, three thousand strong, and what Christian woman ever took an army with her when she went to a husband's arms?

Of all of which Dmitri heard nothing and cared less. Later he did hear. At the moment he was supervising the welcome. The pomp of that is said to have been prodigious. No doubt it was. In the great hall of the palace, a hall heaped to the rafters with bizarre vases and fabulous beasts, there were concerts, masquerades and a state dinner more lavish than anything that anywhere had been known.

Among the courses which, after the oriental fashion, succeeded each other interminably, there were swan's knees, lamb's lungs, roast cygnets, storks cooked in ginger, deer's brains, lemon soup, sweetmeats of honey and attar of rose. Additionally were the wines of Hungary, of Alicante and the Canaries, together with the strong waters of Holland and of France. But these, all of them, after another oriental custom, were served last.

Dmitri had a table to himself, a plate to himself and also a fork, then a great novelty. The table was on a dais. Below and beyond the guests feasted, forkless, from trenchers. Maryna was not present. It was not etiquette that she should be. Nor did she appear until just prior to the ceremony, when old men supported her, as though she were an infant in arms, from the cathedral's entrance to the altar. Dmitri was similarly supported. Etiquette so required. To the assembled Poles it was ridiculous. They laughed indecently.

Afterward, in the Kreml, there was a ball, during which Dmitri, in Polish costume, danced with his bride and, for good measure, with her father. Beyond, in the Red Square, Poles, very drunk, drew their swords, pinked the Muscovites. The good measure was full. Concerts, balls, masquerades, in particular the bride's exhibition of her hair and waist, these things, every one, were pagan abominations. The good measure, full already, overflowed.

To Dmitri and Maryna it was all very rapturous. Life at its apogee had begun. The rapture lasted one week. At the stroke of twelve on the seventh night, men-at-arms, enrolled by Chouiski, were clamouring and beating at the bridal door.

A naked man is never brave, but he may be adroit. Dmitri disappeared through a window. Maryna shrieked, as perhaps only a frightened girl can shriek. Nearby, in an adjoining apartment, were her women. They hurried to her. One of them, the chaperon, was vast and formidable. Under the immense farthingale which she wore, Maryna hid. Just in time. The men had broken in. The other women, who were not at all formidable and who, being Polish, were pretty, were carried away, treated as playthings. Maryna escaped, in a shift, it is said, to her father. The house in which he lodged was besieged. The houses where other Poles lodged were besieged also. They gave as good as was sent. But a lot of them, taken in taverns and the open, were killed outright. To employ an archaic phrase, the streets were dyed—like wool—with blood.

Dmitri, in vanishing through a window, disappeared. For a time, that is. Presently he was found. When found, he had broken his legs. He could not move. In that condition he was shot, stabbed, hacked even in the face, which was disgustingly disfigured. Incidentally he was insulted.

"Dog of a bastard, tell us who you are?"

Dmitri made no reply. He was dead. A wandering Jew had his gabardine torn off. It was put about the naked body, which, carried to the Red Square, was dumped on a table. On that table for three days it remained. On the third night, a thin blue flame hovered above it. The phenomenon, caused probably by the corpse's putrefaction, created a terror all the more profound because superstitious. Who knew what it might portend?

In an effort to ward any evil, the corpse was carried to a cemetery. A grave was dug. The body was lowered into it. Immediately other phenomena occurred. Over the grave, eagles were seen that flew away when approached and then returned. Eagles! At least they were not two-headed. The comfort was meagre. At night, the flame was still visible. What is worse, sounds were heard, oddly discordant, that came, or seemed to come, from below.

The terror augmented. The grave was

DEMETRIUS ✳ IMPERATOR RVSSIÆ MAGNUS DVX MOSCOVIÆ VLODOMER ET NAVOGROD ETC.

The most mightie Prince DEMETRIVS Emperour
of Russia, Great-Duke of Vlodomor, Mosco, and Navogrod: King of Cazan and Astracan, Comaunder
of all Siberia and of the North parts, etc.

Compton Holland excud: F. sculp.

DMITRI

opcned. It was empty! That body had moved.
It had moved of itself! It was at the other
end of the cemetery!

There could be no doubt about it then. The
monkish accusation was recalled. Dmitri was
a sorcerer who knew the infernal art of post-
mortem resuscitation. With a vampire one could
not be too careful. As supreme precaution, the
body was burned and the ashes, rammed in a
cannon, were fired from it. Then only did terror
pass. Dmitri, his ghost or its counterfeit, had
been definitely laid.

Maryna, meanwhile, minus her crown, and
her father, minus his sacks, were extracted from
the besiegers and invited to leave. The invitation was not cordial, but the forms were there.
Polish reprisals, always possible, were, if possible, to be avoided. Hence the civility which
emanated from Chouiski who, in the riot, had
become tsar.

Maryna, calling herself tsaritsa still and insisting on being treated as such, set forth with
the surviving Poles for Sendomir. She never
reached it. The great playwright that destiny
is, had for her an epilogue in reserve. One
may wonder whether, in insisting on her prerogatives, she knew it. Logically, the drama
ended dramatically, as drama should end, on

the bloody night of the interrupted honeymoon.
Did she know that it was to be resumed. One
wonders.

Leo X., a very lettered pope, said and sensibly enough, "Since God has given us the papacy,
let us enjoy it." Chouiski could also enjoy himself. An ignorant and very vile old man, he
was not lettered. But he was capable at least
of a butcher's pleasures and, other things being
equal, he might have supped on them. The
great playwright had planned differently. Before Maryna had gone more than half the way
to Sendomir, a coup de théâtre occurred. That
devil of a Dmitri was alive again!

The news of it, filtering through the Kreml,
struck Chouiski dumb. Reaching the travellers en route for Poland, it stupefied them as
well it might. They looked at the widowed
bride who perhaps was widowed no longer.
Perhaps! It was all highly phantasmagoric.
But in looking they saw that their stupefaction
was not shared by her. She appeared to know
all about it. It may be that she did.

Afterward it was reported that on the bloody
night, Turkish horses disappeared from the
tsaral stables. It was also reported that in the
early morning, a boatman on the Oka ferried
three men, one of whom, indicating another,

said that he was tsar; a statement which he repeated later that day to an innkeeper on the road to Tuchino. In each instance he had added:—"He will return with an army and reward you."

That may or may not have been true. But whether true or false, it was also reported that letters stamped with Dmitri's seal were in circulation. At any rate, a cavalry republic, the Cossacks of the Don, were rising and rallying in his name.

"In his name, yes, but in whose else? Who is this impostor?" Chouiski, with recovered speech, demanded. It was at this juncture, in an effort to show that whoever the reincarnation might be, it was not that of the original tsarevitch, it was then that the wretched old man evolved a lovely expedient. He ordered the young savage's tomb opened and commanded his canonisation. The priests may have wept at the altars, they obeyed.

Dmitri then was at Tuchino. Whether this Dmitri were the prince twice dead, or another being, the reader may take a moment to decide. It had taken Maryna no longer. She hurried to him, threw herself into his virile arms, one of which was longer than the other. It is nowhere related that that malformation had been remarked in Moscow, but it was the peculiarity of the murdered young tsarevitch.

In Tuchino, a bandit's lair, splendour was absent. For balls there were riots; for concerts, brawls. Cossacks drink nobly. The capacity of Poles is proverbial. What is termed the flower of the nobility joined Dmitri in this lair which, camp, lupanar and fortress combined, contained a hundred thousand men, every one of them eager to reseat a tsar, eagerer still to loot the tsaral treasure. Then, presently, off they started.

Chouiski had thought of enjoying himself. Instead he quaked. Sigismond, an army at his heels, was marching on him. Chouiski quaked at that, but far less than he quaked at the demon Dmitri who was marching also. Let the sorcerer again get him and this time farewell to his head.

Against a sorcerer, sorcery is indicated. At Chouiski's orders, magicians worked their spells. Infants unborn were torn from their mothers. From gutted horses hearts were removed. With both a horrible hash was made and strewn, full-handed, as grain is strewn, before the walls. The necromancy succeeded. Abruptly, though through what normal connivance has never clearly appeared, once more Dmitri was assassinated, yet, as was customary with him, briefly only. In the interval, Maryna, carried off by a Tatar, vanished on horseback from history.

The sorcerer reappeared. More exactly, there was another incarnation. Probably the new Dmitri was not Dmitri at all. None the less the avatars continued. The surprising creature never again entered the Kreml, but his ghost was not definitely laid until Chouiski died. That seemed to placate him.

Then leisurely the preludes to another and a greater drama began. Transiently the stage was occupied by Mikhail Romanov, an insignificant insect who, every morning, beat his empty head fifteen hundred times on the stones before the altar. That insect was grandfather of a gorilla.

III

PETER THE GREAT

THE night in which Hercules was conceived lasted forty-eight hours. So at least it has been said. Assuming that the story be true, the night in which Peter was conceived must have lasted twenty-four.

Who the male collaborator may have been is unimportant. But the problem perplexed him. In a scene, tolerably dramatic, which Dolgoroukov recites, he shouted it.

"Whose son am I?" Glaring, he pointed. "Yours, Tihon Streshnief? Speak or I will have you strangled."

Streshnief fell on his knees. "Batushka! Mercy! How can I tell? I was not the only one!"

In the chronicles of nations figures arise. Time passes and they pass with it. They are forgotten like spilt wine. Occasionally come figures that persist. Usually they are brutes. It is the Cæsars that are remembered, not the saints. Cyrillus, a bishop, contrived to be useful and to be beautiful. To be both is to be sublime. Sublimity is a dangerous occupation. It may lead to oblivion and also to Golgotha. Cyrillus gave Russia nothing less than a language. His reward is the dustbin. With the alphabet that he created the name of Petrus Maximus is written. It is written on a page of granite. The granite is red. Voltaire thumbed it and said: "Half hero." Voltaire paused and added: "Half tiger."

A tiger is a beautiful animal. There was nothing beautiful about Peter, nor is there about a gorilla. Peter was a gorilla with brains.

Like the great apes in a Borneo jungle, he sprang and killed. He had the same indisputable instinct for destruction, the same elasticity, the same quick subtlety of sense. In Moor's portrait of him, the expression, vaguely ruminant, is that of a beast that has fed. Back of it is another, an impression of will, inflexible as an axe and of which you feel the chill and the edge. The man is there, framed in wood, like a bird of prey nailed on a panel.

Probably the reincarnation of a Tatar khan, necessarily he was a nihilist. "Take earth and heaven, take all laws human and divine and spit on them and that," said a lucid exponent, "is nihilism." Nihilism and bolshevism differ,

but only in spelling.   Peter was the original bolshevist.

His earliest bath was blood.   At the death of
his mother's husband, surviving enthusiasts
formed opposing factions.   Cheerfully, the
guardians of the peace participated in their massacre of each other.   The spouting blood
drenched Peter; drenched Sophia, his sister;
drenched Ivan, his brother, with whom he had
ascended a two-seated throne.   Back of the
throne was a chair.   Before it hung a curtain,
behind which was the girl.   A moment only.
Sophia was a phantom.   So also was Ivan.   Peter
alone was real.   Watch him!

At his feet Russia sprawled, inert, chaotic; a
land still mediæval, but without chivalry, romance, poetry, troubadours and cours d'amour.
It was a land across which beings moved, ignorant as carps.   Of the mediæval spirit they
possessed only the sure cognition of hell.   Otherwise, its night enveloped them.   They loved it.
Except drink, it was the only thing they did love.
A protection, it made them obscure   See what
he does to them and to it.

As yet he was a cub.   Wait until he grows.
Wait until he becomes, what he did become,
seven feet tall—seven feet which to those beings must have seemed seven hundred.   When

the gorilla was grown, history beheld what the
tired old gossip had never beheld before and
never has witnessed since, the spectacle of a nation, backward, obstinate, rigid, unwilling to develop, tossed from Asia into Europe, knouted
into evolution, terrorised into modernity.

Terror was Peter's nurse. His toys were
weapons. His palace, haunted by nightmare,
was hung with horror. Before him the history
of his house uncoiled in shudders. He gasped,
but only for air. When he stretched his legs,
dwarfs in double rows surrounded him with
screens of violet and concealing silk. Even a
cub would balk at that. When he could, he
got to the sea. Through an atavism proceeding perhaps from the pirates from whom he
presumptively descended, he had dreamed of
it. His predecessors had dreamed also, but they
had fought. There was the Baltic. It belonged
to the Norse. There was the Euxine. It belonged to the Turks. The dream of one or both
was human to the sons of rowers.

In the Kreml, Sophia dreamed not of the sea
but of the sceptre. She wanted it one and in-
divisible in her hand. She wanted to be autocrat. She became a prisoner. Those who had
wanted for her what she wanted were put in
cages and burned alive. Shortly and silently

Ivan disappeared. Peter was sole monarch, lord absolute of everybody, proprietor of Russia, despot of her denizens and destiny, alone on the two-seated throne.

From it he stared at the sea which no other tsar had seen. He determined to cross it, which no other Russian had done. Gautier declared it indecent for a young man to enter the drawing-room of life without a book of verse for boutonnière. Peter felt it unfitting to enter the drawing-room of the world without a victory in his buttonhole. At the time he lacked even a yawl. From abroad he beckoned craftsmen, made a fleet, sailed the Don, attacked Azov, took it.

Then, to see the sights, there started forth a savage, young, tall, dark, grimacing, neurotic, always in a hurry; a lout whom a napkin embarrassed; an oaf whom corsets surprised; a monarch who was a rustic; a potentate who was a clown; a tsar crassly ignorant and aware of it; a man vital, violent, elemental, bestial, drunk every night of his life.

On the part of a Russian subject, travelling was treason. A junketing prince was sacrilegious. Peter who was to kill men with his bare hands, who, while he drank and looked on,

was to order heads off for his amusement, left
clandestinely, incognito, disguised.

Simianly inquisitive, seeing a thousand
things that amazed him, seeing civilisation
which amazed him most, learning in Saardam
how to handle a ship, in London how to handle
a scalpel, in Vienna how to use a fork, assimi-
lating every idea and forgetting none, he learned
how to recruit an army, build a navy, create a
nation and supply it, off hand, by force of edicts,
with a veneer of civilisation that could crack
and did and with a report that startled the world.

The bolshevist was an ape, but ape-artificer.
In occult circles it is said that Victoria R. I. was
formerly Alfred the Great. If that be true,
Peter, prior to becoming a Tatar khan, may
have been Nero, though in that case he had degenerated in the progression.

At Kœnigsburg he asked to see somebody—
anybody—broken on the wheel, a variety of torture which he thought might do for Moscow.
The authorities regretted that they had no avail-
able criminal.

"Here," said Peter, "take one of my suite."

Voltaire had it from Frederick, who had it
from a former envoy, that, one night in Moscow,
Peter amused himself by decapitating twenty
men, drinking flagons of brandy between each

stroke, after which he invited the Prussian representative to try his hand at it. Nero would not have done that; he lacked the energy, lacked the brandy. For the greater glory of Jupiter, he lacked, too, the Prussian.

Subsequently, Peter acquired an interest, unplatonic and brief, in Mary Hamilton, a young woman of Scotch descent, related more or less vaguely to the dukes of that name. Shortly he threw her over. Afterward, as the result of another interest, she had a child and killed it, a very customary proceeding, but to which, in this instance, Peter objected on the ground, perhaps valid, that the child might have become a man whom he could decapitate.

The theatre was prepared. That theatre, the scaffold, was a stage, carpeted with red, hung with black, about which an avid crowd collected.

Mary Hamilton, in white, dressed like a bride, but, in honour of the groom, with black ribbons, was brought there. She was fainting. Peter carried her up the steps, forced her to kneel, looked on at the operation, picked up the bloody head that had rolled on the crimson carpet, gave a lecture on anatomy and the spinal column, eyed the pallid lips which so often had kissed his own, dropped the head, descended the steps, strolled away.

A pleasant person. In the alcove he was equally attractive. There Villebois etched him. "Il était un vray monstre de luxure. Il s'abandonnait à des accès de fureur érotique dans lesquels l'âge et le sexe même luy importait médiocrement."

That was Peter, afterward the Great. At the time he was merely horrible. In the course of the foreign junket, tiresome news reached him from home. Sophia, weary of her prison, but wearier of her demon brother, was urging Moscow to rebel. The budding mutiny was hushed. You might have thought the matter at an end. It had not begun. On Sophia, on Moscow, the gorilla pounced. Corridors of ardent chambers, perfectly equipped with every form of fiendishness, functioned night and day. After preliminary and very agonising delays, those who entered there were burned alive. For others, death was quicker. Ordinary persons were decapitated in coils, at the rate of fifty at a time. Their bodies, carted in thousands beyond the walls, were left to rot. From the balconies of Sophia's prison two hundred hung, as grapes hang, in bunches.

For the greater glory of God, Torquemada

resurrected Moloch and set Castille on fire. For the greater awe of Peter, Moscow was turned into a gehenna. There were groves of gibbets, blood in lakes, hills of dead, tortures vaster than Carthage knew, than Castille beheld. Peter's deputies sank outwearied. Peter was tireless. Axe in hand, he stalked knee-deep in the human abattoir. That axe, dented each night, each morning was resharpened.

Years later, his son confessed a mortal sin. He had hoped his father would die. Commiserately the priest raised a hand. "We all wish it."

Yet no sooner had he gone, than he became Peter the Great, a nation's idol. In Greece, Heraklitos died of laughing, literally of laughing, at the folly of his contemporaries. Heraklitos was then an old man. In Russia, he might have died younger but he would have laughed more.

Peter was a butcher. Also he was tsar. The terms are synonymous. In addition, he was dentist. If you so wished he pulled your teeth. He was quite capable of pulling them any way. He pulled a woman's who did not want him to and who died of it. He attended her funeral. Bon prince, he was practical. He gave Moscow her first hospitals, her first pharmacies and

* cf Merejkowski

kept them busy. In his leisures, which occasionally were spacious, he presided at the Bezpietchalnyi sobor—the council that knows no sadness—an assembly of phallicists whose ceremonies exceeded anything that even the lost books of Elephantis may have told.

From the council that knew no sadness, Peter passed to the council that knew nothing else. Over that also he presided, as over all matters he presided as well. He was the state. He was the living law. Death was his servant. He ordered. Death obeyed.

In the hideous night when Domitian ruled old Rome, informers were at work. Any denunciation, false or true, meant death. On the burg of Peter that night descended. As in Rome, informers were rewarded. For anything, for nothing, the heedless were denounced. On a cellar wall a woman saw, or said she saw, letters traced by an unknown hand in an unknown tongue. The knout! A student in his cups babbled fretfully. The rack! Before the tsar as he passed a drunken peasant lurched. The axe! The arrest of one usually involved the arrest of a dozen. The original culprit, put to the question, shrieked whatever names he could think of. When he could think of no more he was masked, led through the streets, made to point out this one, that one, any one. At sight of him, a cry went up:—"The mask! The mask!" Instantly the streets were empty. In Rome an accused accused his accuser. The latter went mad. That breath of madness blew through the burg that Peter built. "Near the tsar, near death," a Russian proverb runs, and the reign, which was a reign of terror, taught many things, but chiefly how to die—with your nostrils torn out, your eyes extracted, your ears severed, your body beaten into a bag of pulp, or, in the ardent chambers, cremated while yet you lived. God save the tsar!

Resembling no one, intellectually blind and yet intelligent; archroyal and very low, this brute whom fate made despot, destiny made seer. In the nation a force dumb, obscure, but latent, was to elevate it from an insignificant satrapy into an empire wider than the moon at its full. That force recognised itself first in Peter. In the chaos about him, he foresaw the imperialism to be.

The future imperialism is not obvious in the butcher. But it appears in the ogre who dragged from Europe long tatters of her civilisation and forced them down Russia's throat. The ogre will enter in a moment. A soldier comes first.

In Sweden, at that time, stood Charles XII.,

PETER THE GREAT

a man of bronze, a monarch whose kingdom was
not of this world, whose palace was the battlefield and who dressed in war's rich livery of
blood. He had overturned the throne of Poland. He proposed to demolish Peter's, dictate
terms in the Kreml and, from there, take on the
sanguinary and gorgeous East.

He started for Moscow, moving viâ the
Ukraine and Byron's Mazeppa—Hugo's Mazeppa also, Pushkin's as well. It is from a
paragraph in Voltaire's *Histoire de Russie* that
Byron and Hugo evolved their hero who was
a hero, to credulous women, and also to a man
who was not credulous at all.

Peter believed in Mazeppa. He trusted him,
counted on his Cossacks and believed, trusted
and counted in vain. When Charles appeared,
Mazeppa joined him, a treachery that history
damned and poetry absolved. Together they
marched on Peter, beating him on the way so
thoroughly that Peter laughed. It was a lesson. He enjoyed it. "The devils will teach
me to beat them," he shouted and laughed
again. The laugh rang true.

Presently Charles was at Pultowa, the siege
of which a grave historian has stated—and stated
too in that language which only grave historians
employ—"he hotly pressed." The description

is pleasant. The cold was such that crows fell dead. Charles wounded there and delirious from the wound, called to Turks who never heard, to Poles who never came.

Peter did both and so effectively that Charles, delirious still, was carted away, carted afar, carted into obscurity where he died as he had lived, as Roland lived and died, clasping his sole mistress, his sword.

Peter, who had learned his lesson and who had routed what he had not destroyed, sent for the officers taken prisoner.

"Where is your viking?" he asked them. "Where is my brother Charles?

"Keep your swords," he added, "and let me see if you can keep your heads."

That night he got drunk with them, but, more potent than brandy, was the fact that triumphantly he had entered the drama of the world.

Pultowa has its date. That date marks an era. Muscovy, hitherto held down by Swedes, by Poles, by Tatars and Turks, was ready for them all. Heretofore her history had been one long humiliation. At Pultowa she came of age. To celebrate it, Petersburg leaped into being.

A moment before Peter had asked:—"Where are my legions?"

Moscow answered. Moscow pointed to a

long, double hedge of skulls gibbeted there to
remind Russia of the disadvantages of conspiring against him. In Moscow he had massacred
an army.

The troops since recruited were untrained,
unfit. They were sheep. He turned away. In
turning he scattered invitations afar. Tacticians,
drill-sergeants, professors of the art of war, the
surgeons of her clinic, became his guests. Presently, turning back to the sheep, he operated a
transfusion. He put blood in them, mettle, his
own instinct for destruction. Pultowa was the
result and with it a tripled realm, balconies that
overlooked the seas, a proscenium box on Europe, the dominion of the north.

Waliszewski, who has written very passion-
ately about him, says that he had an idea a day.
For a genius that is meagre; for a monarch it
is magnificent; for a Muscovite a miracle. Perhaps Waliszewski exaggerated. Besides, opinions vary as to what constitutes an idea. But
the gorilla had brains. With them he substituted himself for time. The labour of centuries
he effected in years. He tossed the state up, as
skyscrapers are tossed, one storey quick on the
other. From the jimcrack Russia has suffered
ever since. Yet his business was not with the
future. It was with the past which was then

the present, which stuck its tongue at him and which he pulled as he pulled teeth.

It was singular and easy. The creature was a crowned anarchist. More technically, he was an autocrat, which means the same thing. An anarchist wants to do as he likes. An autocrat can—or could. Peter could. He had merely to will and his will was law. He willed that what he thought, all must think: that what he did, all must do. He willed that Russia should dance to his piping, dress to his taste, play the clown, abolish her customs, assassinate her ideals, abjure her gods. He so willed because such was his pleasure. When that pleasure was not gratified instantly, were there misunderstanding, weakness, fatigue, the axe!

The Russian year began September 1st. It began then because on that day, 5508 B.C., God created the world. Nothing could be more authentic. To celebrate the event, everybody fuddled and fought. But nobody smoked. Tobacco was heathen. Nobody danced. In the ascetic orthodoxy of the Russian Church, gaiety was sinful, instrumental music forbidden, learning was damned and ignorance blessed.

Men still wore the long, flowing robes of the East. What women wore is immaterial. When serfs, they were soulless. They did not exist.

Women of the upper class did not appear. Shut away in oriental seclusion, they were invisible. But all men were longly robed and all were bearded. They had to be. In the sacred iconography, Father and Son were bearded and robed. Man, made after the image of God, must be like unto Him. Any dissimilarity was sacrilege.

That sacrilege Peter commanded. In a ukase written with the knout, beards and robes were ordered off, the women were ordered out. Models of what all were to wear and which those who did not wear got the knout until they did, hung in the Red Square. Prior to the knout, robes were torn off at the waist; beards were torn out by the roots. Incidentally men were ordered to smoke. They were ordered to revise their calendar. The year no longer began in the autumn, as it had begun, or in the spring, as it should begin, but after the absurd Roman fashion which Europe had adopted.

With edicts and the lash, the year was revised. Men were shaved, redressed, a pipe was stuck in their mouth, and the beauties of their household were ordered into society in a land in which there was none, had been none rather, for Peter created ballrooms with a ukase. The boiars were pronunciamentoed into entertaining. They were told what to do, what not to do, the days and the hours for it.

No gambling, but dancing was rigorously required. As nobody knew how to dance, Peter personally gave lessons, instructing the sullen beauties that, for the go of it, they must kiss their partners. To encourage them, he ladled brandy in wooden spoons, not forgetting to help himself, becoming in the process as drunk as the ladies, if possible drunker, teaching them not merely the pas de quoi, but the elegancies of deportment and the pomps of etiquette.

Rudiments followed. The bear, taught to dance, was taught to read. He was given an alphabet, partly Greek, partly Bulgarian, which Cyrillus had supplied, which Peter refashioned and which seven-tenths of Russia have not yet acquired. Subsequent autocrats objected to its dissemination. A little learning is a dangerous thing and a lot of it may be revolutionary. Catherine the Greater said that if the inmates of her little household—Russia was her little household—knew how to read, they would write her off. Sensible woman. But she had seen the French Revolution, which to Peter was unimagined. It becomes therefore rather instructive to watch him reaching down into mediæval dungeons, pulling the prisoners into a modern

reformatory, bundling them out of their ideals
into his, kicking over the past with one seven-
leagued boot, projecting them into the future
with the other, tossing them into the mould
from which contemporaneous Russia with her
colossal corruption and volcanic anarchy proceeded.

For university, Russia had the scaffold; for
curriculum, the knout. These things instruct.
They teach the æsthetics of servility, hypocrisy,
smothered hatred and bursting bombs. But not
morals. Peter, devoid of any as an orang-
outang, saw no reason for them. He may have
been right. Mathematics know nothing of
morals. Political economy is not interested in
them. Art ignores them. They are not a prin-
ciple of civilisation. It was not for lack of them
that Rome fell. What sapped her was malaria.
Morals are a luxury and Peter in his catarrhine
ignorance was unaware that the luxuries of life
are its necessities. He wanted the superficial
and the veneered. The tears he sowed to get
them, tsardom reaped.

To Waliszewski, he was the noblest Roman
of them all. He may readily have been that
and remain the perfectly ignoble brute that he
was to his pigmies, for whom, very thanklessly,

he strung balconies from which they could look at Europe and Europe could look at them.

To enhance the view, abruptly, on the Neva —a Tatar word that means mud—there was built, at the cost of two hundred thousand lives, the lives of serfs converted into masons and harried there to death, the town of Petersburg, vast and boreal, where art congealed into tasteless edifices, dreary palaces, empty streets; a city with a heart of stone, a plaster body and extremities of rotten wood.

In Petersburg, Peter made himself emperor, made himself pontifex maximus. Asiatic absolutism, crowned long since, then was mitred. The patriarch had died. Assembled prelates asked him to appoint a successor. "I have," he told them. "I have appointed myself." Lord temporal, lord spiritual, the Antichrist was pope. Besides, why not? The Russias, all of them, everything and everybody in them, were as thoroughly his as the coat on his back. "I will give Russia to whom I see fit," the grandfather of the terrible Ivan unselfishly said. Peter would not merely have said it, he would have done it. He lacked the time. A laundress, handed by a pastrycook, stepped into his shoes.

Louis Napoleon married the granddaughter of a publican. Petrus Maximus married the daughter of a serf. After the manner of an emperor who is above the law, he married her without becoming divorced from a princess, Eudoxia Lapoukhin, already his wife. In the story of the princess there is drama. In the story of the empress there is myth.

The property of a trooper, she passed sidewise and upward to Peter who, for her immediate favours, gave her a ducat. A ducat to the trull to whom he afterward gave a crown! At the time, she had no name. Peter, in addition to the ducat, gave her one. He called her Katinka, also Katierinouchka, a tender diminutive which history severely revised. Historically, she became Catherine I.

In her spiral ascent she reached Menchikov, an ex-pastrycook whom Peter had picked up in the street. Peter made him his mignon, then his minister. When Peter was afar, Menchikov ruled for him. When he was farther, Menchikov ruled alone. It was he who gratified Peter with the lady of the ducat and the crown.

The Margravine of Baireuth, who saw her, said she was short, huddled, tanned, completely lacking in looks, dignity, grace; dressed in a gown covered with dirt and embroidery, and so tricked out with medals, necklaces, gewgaws, that she jingled like a mule.

She had her charms though, a trooper's thirst, the ability to carry her liquor like a boiar and a skill, which no trainer has acquired, the art of taming a gorilla. In her hands a madman was putty. Peter in a rage was a fiend in a fury. Katinka cajoled, commanded and calmed the brute. She lulled him to sleep. When he awoke the access had passed. So are beasts and despots won.

But not detained. Peter had a nostalgia for mud, a homesickness which Katinka shared. Any woman, provided she were ugly and a slattern, could win him and Katinka, empress and entremetteuse, saw to it that he was supplied, not neglecting to provide for her own amusements, gaieties at which Peter did not even shrug his shoulders, except once.

The man, a good-looking young fellow, brother of one of Peter's light o' loves, was chamberlain in Katinka's suite. The position involved duties, among others that of listening to her. In listening, he replied. The conversation was overheard and Peter informed. Ordinarily, the information would not have interested him, but the anonymous letter which conveyed it, stated that the two were conspiring against his life.

The gorilla sprang at the chamberlain who,

at sight of him, fainted. When he recovered, Peter had also. Considerately, sympathetically, with a show of deep affection, Peter assured him that he was sorry, very sorry, but he would have to have him killed.

The theatre was prepared. The avid crowd assembled. Peter took Katinka to see the show. They went there in a sleigh. The day was polar but clear. Katinka remarked about it. That was all. But on her console that night, she found her lover's head.

What turpitudinous, or merely horrible reprisals he meditated for her, one may surmise and never know. Death, whom he had so continuously beckoned for others, took him by the ear. Et ainsi finit l'histoire de Barbe-Bleue.

That was when Katinka was empress. Anteriorly she had children, two in particular, Ann and Elisabeth, one of whom reigned over happy and holy Russia. But Eudoxia the Forsaken, also had a child, Alexis the tsarevitch.

Peter hated them both. They represented the past. By way of contrast, Katinka was the New Woman whom Peter, without going far but low, had found and finding made empress. The paradox of the performance was its inducement. In its vulgarity was its charm. Peter had another in reserve that was to eclipse it, but only in horror.

To approach the latter adequately requires a nearer understanding of Katinka's primitive soul. The slatterns with whom Peter amused himself meant nothing to her. But Eudoxia was very offensive. Eudoxia was noble, she was tsaritsa, she was a saint, or, if not a saint, in the convent where Peter had put her, she resembled one. The insolence of it! A bucket of mud! The bucket was raised, the mud was thrown. Katinka fastened a lover and a conspiracy on her.

The conspiracy was a plot to seize the throne, put the tsarevitch there and abolish the reforms. It was highly imaginative. None the less Eudoxia admitted it, admitted the lover, admitted everything. Beforehand she was knouted. Under the knout even a saint may admit no matter what. Glebov, the lover, an officer and a gentleman, denied everything. The rack could extract nothing from him. On the other hand, a dozen convent nuns said whatever the lash told them to say. The evidence was complete.

Eudoxia was sent to another convent and Glebov to the theatre. At the four corners of the stage were amputated heads. About it were fifty corpses. There Glebov was impaled. On that day the cold was extreme. In order that he might endure the torture as long as possible, he was bundled in furs. During it, Peter gloatingly approached. Glebov spat in his face.

Previously a drama occurred that has never been properly told and now never can be. The proper telling would require the collaboration of Æschylus and Michelet. Here, in cobweb, is the outline.

From the circles of terror that Peter radiated, Alexis shrank. Otherwise, brains and energy deducted, he was Peter's son. His tastes were low. He liked drink and common women. Apart from that, he was inoffensive and, after the manner of the inoffensive, he was ineffective.

Peter always effective and equally offensive, eyed him. What would become of the throne and Russia when both were his? To sit on a throne cannot be difficult. To remain there presupposes strength. Alexis had none. To supply it, Peter bullied him as he bullied everybody, frightened him as he frightened all. He dragged the boy from palace to shambles, from a honeymoon to war. In the same manner that he had put mettle into sheep, he tried to put force into dough. Failing, he exhorted. Failing in that, he threatened. Again he failed. The boy had gone.

The year before he had married a German

girl. The marriage was a precedent. Every
Russian sovereign, except the third Alexander,
who married a Dane, followed that lamentable
example. The girl whom Alexis married was
Charlotte of Wolfenbüttel. Her sister, wife
of the Austrian emperor, was the mother of a
girl, afterward Maria Theresa. Charlotte became the mother of a son, afterward Peter II.
It is said that just before the latter's birth, Alexis
kicked her. It may be true. Peter's court was
a morgue. The amenities were not observed
there. But the classics were taught. One
learned how to suffer and how, too, to disappear.
Charlotte died and was buried. Or so at least
it was announced.

Charlotte lacked beauty. Instead she had the
sentimental form of German sentiment which
was later known as schwärmerei. An officer
tapped at her heart. The green savannahs of
the south, the bayous of Louisiana, called and
beckoned. They got away, went there, loved
there, lived there, left there to go their separate
paths, one of which led Charlotte to Paris, where
she lived on an allowance served to her by her
niece, Maria Theresa.

After Charlotte's death, the Variétés produced a play of which she was the heroine. It
was called *Madame Péterhof*. The play an-

noyed Catherine the Greater. Severely she remarked:—"Everybody knows that the princess
died here of consumption."

A French wit took it up. "Everybody knows
that your husband died of apoplexy."

Before Charlotte's fantasia began, Alexis had
left her. He fled from the morgue in disguise.
Years earlier, Peter had also fled in disguise.
He fled to escape his ignorance. Alexis fled to
escape that ignorance which still persisting made
Peter blind to the fact that, potent though he
were, for the power he misused he would render
account, not to a recording angel perhaps, but
to himself. In Avitchi, the plane that the very
vile enter when they have passed from here, the
penalty of the damned consists in beholding
what they have done. Here they may have
lacked a conscience, they acquire one there; acquire, it may be, two of them. If there is a word
of truth in what occultism tells of that plane,
Peter must have acquired three consciences, six,
a dozen. He needed them all.

At the time he had none whatever. Katinka
had none either, but she had just had a child.
Maternity prompting, she prompted Peter.
Alexis was invited to become a monk. Alexis
agreed. He had to agree. He had no choice.
But then the cowl is not nailed to the head.

Peter gone, he could discard it, ascend the throne and abolish the reforms. The reforms meant little to Katinka, but the throne meant all. It was in these circumstances that she fastened on Eudoxia a conspiracy which involved Alexis. Peter would have killed him. Before he could, Alexis had gone.

At once the magic circles of terror expanded. Peter was seeking him, willing him back.

Furtively the boy crouched and scurried. With him, crouching and scurrying also, was another boy whom he called his page. The description shows imagination. The boy was a girl and a serf whom he had garnered, as Peter gathered Katinka, on the backstairs of life. Her name was Euphrosine. She was a Finn and looked it. She had the expression, slightly bestial, that Finns display. Alexis loved her. The little animal enraptured this lad in whose life raptures had been scant. Together they got down to Vienna where they hid and dreamed. But that is an exaggeration. Alexis dreamed dreams which Euphrosine dreamed for him— Peter dead, the abolition of the reforms, Alexis tsar, Euphrosine empress!

As for that final touch, why not? What had Katinka been? Longly the boy discussed the dreams which, ambrosia to her, were nectar to

him, but on her account only.   Left to himself,
his dream would have been a country boiar's existence, quiet, sensual, drunken.

But the flaming circles were contracting and
they fled again, this time to Naples where Peter's
huntsmen, who for a year and a day had been
stalking, quarried them.   The shudder that
shook Alexis then was Æschylean.   Yet how
needlessly!   There was a letter, very reassuring,
from Peter.   Alexis had only to return; everything would be forgiven, his father's tenderness
restored.

Peter added:—"If you refuse, I, as your
father, will curse you and, as your sovereign,
condemn."

On reaching Vienna, Alexis had gone to the
emperor.   Charles VI. was his brother-in-law.
The tenuous bond appealed.   Charles promised
to look after him and, when Alexis fled to Naples, he told the viceroy there to have an eye on
him also.   But Peter, who knew what he wanted
and knew, too, how to get it, was massing troops.
The viceroy did not want war, nor did Charles.
When Alexis in his terror invoked the one, then
the other, they threw him to the dogs.   Alexis
might still have escaped.   But Euphrosine who
expected to be another Katinka and to replace

her, persuaded him to bargain that Peter should consent to their marriage.

Tenderly Peter yielded. Only, in view of tsaral customs and Alexis' rank, the marriage must be solemnised in Moscow.

Off then they went under guard of that tender father's huntsmen, a guard that, for Alexis at least, was never relaxed until that tender father's will was done.

In Moscow, in the great hall where the terrible Ivan throned, the terrific Peter questioned. Alexis, shaken and swooning, had nothing to say except that he was a devoted son. It was a lie, one which, no doubt, the Lords of Karma remitted.

Then came the turn of Euphrosine, a chance for the antique virtues, the display of Cornelian traits. Not a bit of it. The little trull, whose ambitions had been privately disabused, unwound the thread of her lover's dreams—tsardom and the reforms abolished!

Face to face with Alexis, eye to eye as it is expressed in the Muscovite code, she was sentencing him to death. He knew it, yet more profoundly afflicted by the treachery of the creature whom he still adored than by any torture that his father could inflict, he collapsed.

Peter was most gracious to the skirted Judas.

He gave her a dowry and married her to an officer with whom, it is said, she lived very happily.

In the eyes of gods that see and foresee, Alexis fared better. He was murdered.

On that day the stage was bare. The usual properties, the red carpet, the black draperies, the knout, the rack, the knife, the block, the axe, these things were absent. The theatre was closed. The blood of kings is sacred. A tsarevitch could not be butchered to make a Russian holiday.

In a cellar beneath a cellar, a pillared vault lit by torches that were sometimes human, Alexis was beaten into insensibility, drenched with salted water, revived, beaten again, longly torn, considerably burned, killed thoroughly.

Peter, twitching neurotically, biting and moistening his lips, heard his son's shrieks, watched him die. Whether he delivered the usual post-mortem lecture, history does not say. What she does say is that on the morrow, which was the anniversary of Pultowa, he laughed, danced and made merry.

Nero killed his mother. Her crime was in giving him birth. But, monster though he were, the monstrosity of his own crime haunted him. Ivan who, in monstrosity, was his equal, killed his son and wept. Alessandro Borgia, their peer, assembled the consistory, beat his breast, vomited his incests, purged, or tried to purge, his hideous soul. Peter, more monstrous than those three monsters, killed his son and made merry. But that is not his epitaph.

In his contempt of every decency, in the edicts with which he changed the status of things, in his obliteration of national customs, he assassinated the ideal. That is his epitaph.

In constructing, he undermined. In correcting, he corrupted. Russia's rottenness proceeded from his knout; her anarchy, from his autocracy.

Peter garroted the past; already Ivan had strangled the future—dual felonies that put Russia in a sociological fourth dimension, a plane abnormal, apart, where lurked and brooded the forces elemental that were to scatter the eagles, destroy the state, startle the world.

Peter and Ivan were the obstetricians of anarchy's posthumous accouchement, though probably long before, on spheres beyond our ken, it was pre-ordered that they should be. After the manner of geological transformations that seem cataclysmic but which are beneficent, probably they were the gestators of a Russia yet to be.

IV

IMPERIAL SABLES

PETER knouted his wife, killed his son, beheaded his mistress. He was a great man. After the funeral, opéra bouffe. On the throne sat a laundress, put there by a pastrycook.

At no time, anywhere, except in Haiti, has there been anything as impudent. From a Haitian revolution a slave emerged emperor. The slave was Soulouque. He could not read, he could not write. But he could make his mark and he did and a very dirty one. The laundress was quite as scholarly. Balzac planned a play about her and gave it up. It was too much for him. Previously, Grétry presented her in an opera. The colouring of the score was as suited to her as a piano is to a kitchen. Perhaps only Offenbach, who turned melody into a strumpet, could have succeeded with her. In that case and by comparison, the *Grande Duchesse de Gerolstein* would be opera seria.

Peter's reign was a perpetual martyrology. The reign of his widow was an uninterrupted de-

bauch. The one modern parallel is Rabelais'
vastes lippées. Miraculously the empire persisted, its might increased. In conditions practically identical the same phenomenon occurred
in Rome. But the circumstances of the Latin
miracle are clearer than the Slav. Russia lacked what Rome possessed, a Suetonius to describe,
a Tacitus to judge. To fill the picture there is
little else than the dispatches of foreign legates.
In one of these dispatches the government is
called a chaos and the court a bordel.

Death in taking Peter by the ear, took him so
abruptly that he had no time to appoint a successor. Legally, if the term had any meaning
and it had none, the indicated heir was his grand-
child, the son of the murdered Alexis, or, in de-
fault of the latter, an illegitimate daughter, or
else a more legitimate niece. The complications that these people subsequently effected
would be farcical were it not for the tragedies
that ensued. But after the good old Roman
fashion, in prevention of any complications and
while Peter was still rattling at death, Katinka
subventioned the pretorians. With the guards
behind her, the rest was easy and Menchikov,
who had superintended the subventioning, attended to that.

Menchikov entered history from the gutter,

Katinka from a wash-tub. The daughter of Livonian serfs, she was fat, coarse and a laundress. During the siege of a tottering town, where she practised her genteel vocation, she got ifrom under the crashing walls and crawled in among Peter's troopers. One of them took her, beat her, turned her over to a sergeant, who passed her up to a lieutenant, from whom she passed to a captain. From him, on the escalator of fate, she reached Menchikov, who gave her to Peter, who gave her a ducat and added a crown.

Inconvenient preludes deducted, there, retold, would be the tale of the darky beggar-maid and the African king Cophetua, were it not that the negress did not live to reign and the laundress did.

Katinka, Peter called her, for he had to call her something and she had no name of her own. In spite of which and with no other imaginable attraction than the manner in which she washed soiled linen, this wench who had sprung from the mud and who fell back there, became Catherine I., Autocrat of All the Russias. There is no parallel for that, even in mythology.

In an old print, Peter is shown, looking up from a table covered with dishes and bottles, while Menchikov leads the lady in. The picture is suggestive and probably exact. But Menchikov after leading her in did not back himself out. For a year and a day she remained the property of both.

There is no immaculate history. If there were it would relate to a better world. The maculacy of these people exceeds the powers of decent prose. None the less it has been a subject of wonder that an emperor could have gone the extravagant length of marrying a laundress. Perhaps the extravagance was the incentive. In Peter's mind, and he had one, the marriage may have served to convey the expression of his supreme contempt for everybody and everything. It is difficult to imagine how he could have made it more emphatic. But apart from that snap of the finger, there was another reason, one already indicated and perhaps more profound. The demon that he was she could transform into a child. On his horrible soul she poured balm.

Behind the balm was a gold mine. In the perpetual funeral that Peter conducted, she interceded. At her prayers, penalties were remitted. Those prayers she sold. For the intercession she was paid. Boiars sentenced for a yes or a no to the scaffold, sent her bags of coin. Their pardon followed. The bags were many and in time very useful. It was with them that she subventioned the pretorians who, Peter gone, secured for her the throne.

In these enterprises she was prompted and aided by Menchikov who, like her, could neither read nor write. He was otherwise educated. In the hard school of a harsh court, and previously in the training camp that the gutter is, he had learned how to want and, what is superior, how to get what he wanted. Originally apprentice in a sweetshop, Peter picked him up in the street, debauched him and, afterward, made him prince of the empire, a Slav grandee with titles by the yard, lord of domains of which the enumeration would fill a page.

The meal was insufficient. His appetite grew as he ate. A rapacious brute with a strapping figure and a bold and fumbling eye, he wanted the throne and got it; nearly, that is, for Peter gone he was practically tsar and, when Katinka had followed her gorilla, he was regent. Nor was that enough and reasonably perhaps since regency is not heritable or even permanent. Katinka's successor was Peter's grandson, then a boy, and that boy he determined should marry his daughter. Meanwhile he filled his pockets, already replete, stuffing them with gigantic confiscations, becoming in the process despotic as Peter, greedy as Ivan, with—what unfortunately both of them missed—destitution for climax and Siberia for finale. But no, that was not the end. After being prince, generalissimo, regent, the scoundrel became sublime. Despoiled, degraded and in chains, he grew fat!

Prior to that astounding coup de maître, and immediately after he had placed his chattel on the throne, it was his custom to go to her, before she was up, and ceremoniously salute her.

"Ouray, Katinka! What shall we drink?"

The question decided, he fuddled with her and whomever she had at her side. Generally, the third party was some one whom he had never seen, or she either, until the day before. The high and puissant lady held reviews that she might make her choice. Always exclusive, usually she was drunk. Her reign, in consequence, while not brilliant historically, socially was delightful. It established a precedent which her immediate successors scrupulously observed.

Among these was her daughter, Elisabeth. Waliszewski said that, in following her mother's example, she used her own bed as spring-board to the throne. Apparently that is true. A regiment of her lovers put her there. But that was after she had already refused it and for a reason delicate, perhaps, but commendable. At the time, a poet compared her to a goddess on a cloud. The comparison will be presently examined. The only comparison that could fit her mother would be one that likened her to a scullion on a dais. The woman was nothing else and to her credit did not pretend to be. With no fear of another severed head confronting her, gluttonously she reassembled and wallowed in the mud from which she had sprung.

At fifty, her health ruined by the cups of dirt and vodka of which avidly she drank the deeper as her strength decreased, it became obvious that she would soon rejoin her gorilla and it was in these circumstances that the succession was offered to Elisabeth who, for a reason that will be recited, refused.

There remained her sister, who had married a Holsteiner that nobody wanted and whom everyone got, later on that is, in the shape of his whelp, an ignoble poodle, husband of Catherine the Greater. But meanwhile and additionally there was the son of the murdered Alexis, an agreeable lad with an agreeable minority ahead of him. Katinka appointed him tsar, with Menchikov for regent.

The lad's style and title was Peter II. Apart from the title, his style was good. He said, or was said to have said, that Vespasian would be his model, that no one should leave his presence depressed.

Wide-eyed, Petersburg commented and marvelled. Centuries earlier, the astonishment of Rome had been as vast. Behind Vespasian stretched a line of imperators that dispensed death as readily as Ivan and Peter. But they dispensed it with an urbanity which Muscovy never knew. Greece humanised the Cæsars, Tartary brutalised the tsars. The Cæsars invited men to die. The invitation was civil. It put the recipient at his ease. It left him free to choose whatever death displeased him least. Occasionally, to fatten fish, a slave was tossed in a pond. To flatter the plebs, occasionally a senator was thrown in the arena. Now and then a seer might be punished as Epictetus was, by having a leg broken. But to a Roman citizen, torture was never applied. Rome assimilated many an orientalism but not that, and it was in that that the tsars exceeded the Cæsars.

Petersburg marvelled consequently at the young emperor's benignity which, however, did not extend to Menchikov.

Menchikov was his master, his task-master, his ruler, his regent, his autocrat, precisely as he was despot of all the Russias. The tyranny of it irked the young tsar, already embarrassed by

Menchikov's daughter, a young woman with the cold eyes of a ghoul. At the time, Menchikov was decorating the streets with columns topped with spikes. On the spikes were heads. From the columns rotting corpses hung.

Peter II. ordered them removed. With that gesture he asserted himself. With the columns, Menchikov fell. Convicted of counterfeiting and embezzlement, petty felonies on a grand scale that he must have committed for practise merely, from the apex of power, from the summit of wealth, without one thing to his name, except the clothes on his back and the chains on his feet, he went to the great white house of the dead that Siberia was and where, superior to destiny, his girth increased. That was superb. He was otherwise magnificent. Already he had founded a line, unique in history, a race of male Pompadours.

Petersburg, savage but timorous, relished the tyrant's vast dégringolage and savoured the young emperor's promise.

The first to remind him of it was his aunt, Elisabeth. Waliszewski says that she marred the lad's ingenuousness. Another Cherubino one might think. But the melodious problem, *Che cosa e amor?* he had already investigated. More Valois than Romanov, he was a Muscovite

Henri III. He had all the feminisms of that king who contrived to be queen. From his aunt he learned nothing, except that love is a pathological condition, from which a tsarevna's convalescence may be immediate. Elisabeth, too distrait to prolong the lesson, abandoned the lad, who became engaged to a Dolgorouki girl, with whose brother, Alexis, he had entered the hermaphroditisms of Valois nights.

The Dolgoroukis were highly noble, so noble that when, long later, Alexander II. married one of the house, it was said, and very correctly, that the princess was marrying beneath her. The second Alexander was not a Romanov. The tribe was then extinct. The last of the litter was Elisabeth's daughter. But the Dolgoroukis of this epoch were perhaps less fastidious than they afterward became.

At the ceremonies of the betrothal, and very gorgeous they are said to have been, a ghost materialised. The ghost was Eudoxia Lapoukhin, Peter's first wife, whom he had knouted and whose lover he impaled. From a convent where ceaselessly she prayed, she came in the antiquated, barbaric and radiant robes of a Muscovy tsaritsa. Psychic from long vigils and very pale, this phantom of the past who, during the reign of a trull, had been too lofty to descend,

PETER II

vacated the cloister, reappeared on earth, blessed
her grandson and silently, sadly, royally, her
glowing robes about her, drew back from before
a drama which, it may be, her psychic eyes foresaw.

The fiancée's immediate family consisted of
her father, her uncle, and her brother Alexis,
with whom she lived in a great palace and in
equal pomp. The girl had red hair, red lips,
a cameo profile, passionate and proud, but not
too proud. Those lips had met other lips and so
lingeringly that the result became apparent.

The inconvenience of the situation was complicated by the boy tsar. At the time he was
living in the Dolgorouki residence. There he
developed typhoid. It was thought that he
would die and, what is worse, too soon.

An effort was made to hasten the marriage.
The boy was delirious. An attempt was made
to have him sign a ukase appointing the girl his
heir. The boy was unconscious. An expedient
which then suggested itself was to put the girl
in his bed and announce that he had honoured
her with his permission to be there, after having,
in his quality of pontifex maximus, performed
the marriage himself. There was still another
way, perhaps superior: since the lad could not
sign the ukase, why not sign it for him?

In the vast palace, in the dead of night, feverishly these people turned from one plan to another, uncertain how to act, certain only that if they did not act and act immediately, the throne was gone. In the jeopardy of that, the ukase was signed and not a moment too soon. A minute later the boy emperor was dead. It was the girl's brother who signed the ukase. Dropping the pen, he drew his sword and rushed out with the cry, "Live the empress!"

The cry found no echo. The forgery was never employed, though, through what connivance is uncertain, it was discovered. The dead boy's betrothed went to Siberia. En route, a demand was made for the engagement-ring. Haughtily she extended her hand:—"Cut it off and the finger with it."

Her brother went to the scaffold. There, while his arms and legs were being broken, he is represented as reciting a prayer, scanning each word from beginning to end. The story is not improbable. The same thing occurred in London, at Smithfield, which Mary Tudor turned into a Plaza Mayor and where she exceeded the Inquisition.

Meanwhile, the nightmare throne was vacant. Official caretakers dusted it and wondered about the next occupant. In wondering, they thought

of Peter's nieces, the daughters of his brother
Ivan.

Ivan had no daughters. Always less than half
a man and never more than half a sovereign,
when Peter shoved him aside, he wandered, a
lost soul, into the country where he lived dis-
mally, in shabby state and where his wife had
two children, both girls, neither of whom was
his, yet who, none the less, were born in wedlock,
a formality which Peter, in regard to his own
daughters, had imperially omitted. The more
legitimate nieces remained. One had married
the duke of Courland; the other a Mecklenburg
prince. This other will appear in a moment.
The Courlander comes first.

Pink, fat, large and greasy, she was familiarly
known as Big Nan, except to Carlyle who, with
easy humour, called her a Westphalia ham. Her
husband died the day after the wedding, not of
delight, but of the nuptial feast, during which
he gorged and gulped gargantually. For after-
course there were pastries, from which nude pigmies sprang and danced, an entertainment that
may have excited his further and fatal efforts.

Big Nan survived and became empress, a rôle
which the world has generously forgotten. But
also she became a figure in a romance which the
stage recalls.

Nan's minor part occurred at Mittau, the capital of Courland where, as duchess, she held court. It is said that she never bathed. In her day, Russian women of position washed in decoctions of roots mixed with brandy which afterward they drank. It is said of this lady that she preferred melted butter. It is also said that she had a negligent cook hanged where she could watch his last wriggles. At table, her women were beaten before her. Their screams gave her an appetite.

At Mittau, she had other distractions. She liked gossip and tales of brigands. These at an end, she turned to her chamberlain, whose wife discreetly retired.

The chamberlain, Bühren, who afterward variously mutilated, exiled and killed over a hundred thousand people, was a German. Previously there had been another German and it was intermediately that a romance occurred on which Scribe built a play in which Rachel appeared, not as Big Nan, but as Adrienne de Lecouvreur, actress and chère amie of Maurice de Saxe.

Men do not dream any more as that man lived. The son of Augustus of Poland and of Aurore of Kœnigsmarck, he became marshal of France, fought on every battlefield and posthumously in

that of letters.   George Sand was his descendant.   He had fought at Pultowa.   He had
fought before, he fought again, in a series of
conflicts which amours and revels distended.
When he was dead, men sharpened their swords
on his tomb.   When he lived, women contended
for him.   Among these were the Duchesse de
Bouillon and Adrienne de Lecouvreur.   In a
duel that they fought for him, the duchess poisoned the actress.

Mozart had not then appeared.   Molière had
and with him Don Juan.   The latter pre-existed
the playwright.   Protean, indefinite, eternal, the
oldest and the youngest man on earth, Maurice
de Saxe was one of his many avatars, perhaps
also an avatar of the Cid.   Reprobate and pal-
adin, the story of his conquests, carried from one
metropolis of pleasure to another, reached
Petersburg and passed thence to Mittau, where,
a troop of henchmen at his heels, but always gallant, he came to claim the duchy.

The sinews of the enterprise had been furnished by Adrienne.   It used to be said that a
gentleman may receive gifts only from his mistress and his king.   Adrienne, all in all for her
lover, sold her jewels, melted her plate.   It was
on the proceeds that the beau sabreur appeared
at Mittau.

Immediately Big Nan was his. In addition, he could have had the duchy. In addition to the duchy he could have had an empire. Nan wanted him to marry her. The duchy was in his hand, the duchess in his arms, the empire in her pocket. But not every one can sup on Westphalia ham. A slice or two sufficed. Maurice took to reading *Don Quixote,* a pastime in which he was surprised by one of Nan's ladies.

At the time, the palace was dark. It was darker when the surprise ended. Maurice undertook to carry the lady to her own apartment. On the way, a watchman saw them, saw rather what he imagined was a two-headed ghost, shrieked with fright and dropped his lantern. Maurice kicked at the lantern, tried to extinguish it, slipped in the effort and fell with the lady on the watchman who shrieked the louder. A door opened. It was Nan's. She threw a glance out, followed it and raised the lantern. A page of history turned. It was in turning it that Nan consoled herself with Bühren.

Bühren was the son of an ostler, a circumstance which elucidates a contemporary remark that he talked to horses like a man and to men like a horse. Otherwise he was of the Pompadour lineage which, founded by Menchikov, was to continue on to Potemkin. Casanova, who met him, as he met everybody, says that he was finelooking. So is a vulture. Nan made him duke, changed his name from Bühren to Biron and, with enviable imagination, evolved a genealogy that interrelated him with one of the first families of France. When the head of that family heard of it he laughed and asked:— "What better name could the canaille have chosen?" But all that was insufficient for this German who could not speak Russian and still less French.

Nan, at the time, was empress. Ignorant, indolent and cruel, she resembled the serpent painted by Raphael that had a woman's head. Bühren had the head of a bird of prey. Otherwise they were admirably mated. Both possessed that dangerous characteristic which stupidity is. Nan, in creating him duke of Courland, made him premier of Russia. But the Menchikov lesson taught him nothing except the impermanence of delegated power. By way of insurance against the hazards of the morrow, he conceived the easy expedient of marrying his daughter to the Holstein whelp whom Catherine the Greater afterward married and murdered. But in his wheels there were spokes, put there by Ostermann and Munnich, generals who had come down from Peter, and who had plans of their own concerning him and that daughter of his, pleasant plans with Siberia among them. Bühren, meanwhile, a Pompadour tsar, was peopling that land, sending citizens there in droves or, more expeditiously, to the scaffold. The orgy appealed to him vastly.

The court then was charming. Under Peter it had been a morgue. Under Katinka, an assignation house. Nan, with Bühren and his discreet wife for managers, elevated it to the dignity of a tap-room. "Here!" a chamberlain called at an officer who neglected to get drunk. "Don't you know that your conduct is insolent? You are her majesty's guest."

In Peter's day the court was bare. In Katinka's it was filthy. Under the Bühren management it became an oriental cabaret, glittering and tawdry.

On a throne in a great gaudy room, lolled Frau Bühren, duchess of Courland. Humpbacked and hideous, she was royal. The robe she wore a couturier valued at a hundred thousand roubles. Her jewels were worth two million. In lolling, she smiled and very fondly at her children who, in their romps, threw ink about. Let the darlings play! With whips they lashed the boiars. Who ever saw such dears?

Adjacently were jesters, dwarfs, crippled

princes that played the clown, swarms of attendants in all the costumes of all the Russias and a greater swarm of Germans. The court was German. The government was German. The orgy was Teuton. Only the boiars converted into clowns and cripples were Slav. But clowns can think, cripples can hate. At the moment, with heads that shook, uncertain how long they would own them, they knelt. Along the walls, in gilded cages, were nightingales, larks, canaries, thousands of them. From the doorway, two generals peered and muttered.

In another room lay Big Nan. The tales of brigands that she used to like, pleasured her no longer. Bühren had made her live them. Beside her, the vulture perched. Nearby were three other Germans, the prince and princess of Brunswick and their child, a boy.

The princess, daughter of the duchess of Mecklenburg, was Nan's niece. The boy was next in line. In the drama of Russian history, his history is unique. It must wait on the romance of his father and mother, an admirably assorted couple who never spoke. A grave historian remarked of Louis XV., qu'il fit à sa femme sept enfants sans lui dire un mot. The Brunswick pair, equally reserved, were less prolific. The boy sufficed.

The girlhood of the princess had been var-
iegated by a duo with a man named Lynar.
Why he consented to sing with her seems mysterious. An equivocal young person with classic
inclinations, she was plain, vain and stupid.
Presently, as a result of the duo's lilt, she was
married to an imbecile. Subsequently this boy
was born. Big Nan being childless, the happy
family was invited to the annex of Berlin that
Petersburg had become and where the mystery
of Lynar's civility was dissolved. About the
otherwise avoidable mädchen he had foreseen
the sables. What Bühren was to the aunt, he
might become to the niece and, as it happened,
he did.

A few years later, the greater Catherine
etched him:—"A fine looking fellow, with the
dress and the airs of a fop, I hear he sleeps in a
complexion mask and boasts of eighteen children." Catherine added details, graphic certainly, but not in conformity with present taste.
That is hardly to her discredit. Formerly, prelates employed in the pulpit expressions which
to-day a coster would avoid.

In the interim, affairs of state occurred. Big
Nan, overcome by drink, took to her bed. The
extreme unction was suggested. "Don't fright-
en me," she irritably retorted. But death was

eyeing her. It may be she did not know it. Bühren did. So also did the Brunswickers whose complete nullity appealed to him. Since their boy was to be tsar, he saw no reason why the curtains of Nan's alcove should not be modelled for him into a robe of sables. He prepared a ukase to that effect.

"Do you want to be regent?" Nan asked. Those were her last words. She signed the ukase. That was her final gesture.

The gesture was a signal. The clowns and cripples who could think and hate prepared to act. But already two generals, long since prepared, were acting.

It had been Bühren's ambition to be regent. He gratified it for twenty-two days and expiated it for twenty-two years. On the twenty-second night of his regency, his daughter, a lass quite as lovely as her discreet mamma, woke to sudden cries. In an adjoining room, her father, half naked, was struggling with grenadiers whom the two generals, Ostermann and Munnich, commanded. Bühren, knocked on the head, was carried senseless to the street, where his wife and daughter, both in chemise, were carried with him.

The next day, charged with having attempted the life of the late empress by taking her to drive in the rain, he and his started for a prison which Munnich had personally designed and which later, the designer occupied with him.

It was Elisabeth who put him there and Oster-mann also.   Meanwhile the little palace revolution had succeeded.   Nominally, the Brunswick woman ruled.

Ann of Mecklenburg and of Brunswick was as vacuous as Big Nan, in addition to being more indolent.   With weak gestures she trailed the sables that Nan had bedrabbled.   Perhaps less Mecklenburg than Mytilene, her tastes, such as they were, were exotic.   Apart from Lynar, she had companions of a category that Brantôme ignored and Kraft-Ebbing described.   Through her brief paragraph in history, she moved languidly to Lesbian airs.

To Petersburg that mattered little.   The woman's regency was objectionable but not at all on that account.   The reigns that preceded hers had inured to anything, no matter what.   It was the deepening German atmosphere that annoyed.   The woman was half German and her child, Ivan VI., Mecklenburg on her side and Brunswick on his father's, was German to the core.   There was some one else who was not German, some one who was Russian through and through.   But also there was the scaffold.

Subterraneanly a conspiracy was formed that, silent at first, confined to a few, presently showed its teeth.   One night, to the clatter of arms, the Brunswick woman awoke.   Elisabeth stood before her.

V

THE NORTHERN MESSALINA

QUINTILLIAN said that history and poetry are sisters. He was dreaming. Yet that dream of his Elisabeth exemplified. To-day her face, her figure, her reign are vague. In the great penumbra she has greatly faded. Vers libre remain. They tell of a woman who beat the fat Frederick to his knees, nearly crushed the egg from which Bismarck hatched a Kaiser, and whose many loves were briefer and more burning than the wick of her alabaster lamp. They tell of a war-woman who was a lady of pleasure.

The housemaids of history have tidied her alcove, burnished her morals and locked the door. Excellent method. Elisabeth, who had a grain of humour, would have enjoyed it. It is quite in accordance with her own ideas which she entirely neglected to observe. If she had a broom, she did not use it and she left her door wide open. To look in on her is not good manners. Real history never had any.

Nor had she. Ignorant, irascible, cruel and, in her later years, always drunk, autocratically she did as she liked. A great privilege, it was part of the orgy, the best part. Without it the feast would have had no savour, the wine no taste. It enabled her and the rest of the lot to do things for which there are no words in any dictionary and no penalty in any code.

Lomonosov, a poet of her day, compared her to a goddess on a cloud. Well, yes, perhaps. But she was a trifle heavy for it. The earth appealed to her more than the sky, more even than the throne which was offered to her and which, for a delicate reason, she refused. Engaged at the time in a fervent amour, she feared the ceremonial would interrupt it. A young woman so retiring was bound to win hearts and she did by the regimentful. Besides, her mind was as changeable as her affections. In addition she was Peter's daughter. Over and above all she was Russian.

One night, a corps of grenadiers, laughing mightily at the adventure, carried her, laughing also, to the palace, where she pulled the regent out of bed, sent her and hers to the devil and, in the same lively manner, ran up the steps of her father's throne.

The fashion in which her reign began must

have interested Sardou.   During the Brunswick
management, during that also of Big Nan, many
people, but two in particular, had been thought-
less enough to annoy her.   The two she ordered
broken on the wheel.   The stage with its red
carpet and black draperies was prepared. Avidly
the crowd assembled.   Munnich, in full uniform, a scarlet cloak about him, a smile for every
one, a nod to those he knew, gallantly ascended
the steps, threw off his cloak, partially un-
dressed and, still with that smile, listened while
he was told that torture had been commuted to
decapitation.   Then, just as the axe was raised,
more theatricals.   Instead of decapitation, exile.

To the crowd's immense disgust, Ostermann
was treated similarly.   Both went to Siberia.
Hundreds   followed   them.   The   hundreds
became thousands.   The thousands multiplied.
Before Elisabeth died she recalled them all, all
that still lived that is, except two.   These were
women.   How and why they went will be told
in a minute.

Elisabeth was very beautiful.   She knew it
and it delighted her.   She loved life, loved
pleasure, loved her beauty best.   Time had the
impertinence to touch her.   Her beauty departed.   At that, this sovereign whom admiration had lifted, like a divinity, to the skies, could

THE EMPRESS ELISABETH

not, as a mortal might, fall from them. A goddess still, she disappeared.

When a girl and a beauty, there was question of her becoming queen of France. The idea, originally Peter's, Versailles considered and, other things being equal, a Russian instead of a Pole might have been the thrice-blessed wife of Louis XV. But Elisabeth had not been born in the pomps of matrimony. It was afterward that Peter married her mother. In the eyes of legitimate France, Elisabeth was illegitimate. That was sufficient. There was more. Elisabeth, who even as a lass loved life, dressed like a man and hunted hyenas and lovers.

Her first affair, a Slav eclogue, was with a shepherd whom she pursued and overtook. Very presuming of him, none the less. To teach him the respect due to a tsarevna, his tongue was cut out. Along the tundras of the Siberian coast, thereafter he meditated on that lesson.

The shepherd was succeeded by a tenor, the tenor by a regiment. Highly temperamental, Elisabeth changed her chosen only less frequently than her costumes, of which, in the course of her volatilely voluptuous reign, she accumulated nineteen thousand, together with a few less than five thousand pair of shoes. Incidentally there was a child. About Elisabeth romance clung.   About the child there is tragedy.   That also will be told in a moment.

In the long illness that Russian history is, the romance of the woman and of her reign relaxes. Set between the hysteria that had gone and the relapses to come, the pages of the imperial annals turn to airs that are almost blythe, to a gaiety sickly but convalescent.   From windows that gave to the south and west, the patient beheld defeats and massacres.   The defeats were those of Frederick the Pseudo-Great; the massacres, those of Prussians.   Medicaments like these invigourate.   Accompanying them were gusts of culture, a trifle uncertain, the hesitant preludes of freer life.   Heads were still shaky.   They were no longer cut off for a yes or a no.

These restoratives were apprehensible from the upper storeys only.   Beneath them, the soul of the nation, narcotised at birth, slept restlessly. Sleep was Russia's normal condition.   No European nation slept longer.   Peter shook her, kicked her to her feet, put her at work.   Russia laboured at his bidding, toiled beneath his lash, writhed on his rack and, he gone, fell asleep again.   Conscious she was but conscious of nightmare.   She knew that she agonised but how or why she could no more tell than a child with the croup.   The subsequent shrieks of the Terror, the amputations of the austere guillotine, the festivals and convulsions of France, passed her unheeded. Somnambulistic, automaton, hypnotised by absolutism's basilisk stare, night held her and continued to hold her until the Crimeañ war.

The shock of that ignoble scramble stirred her. From her cot that was at once a cage and a coffin, she showed a few poisoned fangs, but only to have them drawn. They have grown afresh since then. Since then, from being affrighted, she frightened the world. But meanwhile her brain was still heavy, her pulse was slow. She suffered without knowing why. Time, the great pathologist, was occupied elsewhere. Even otherwise, it is not until a nation can diagnose her own maladies that the indicated remedies are applied.

They were not applied then. On the upper storeys of the hospital, a pale daylight fell. Elsewhere, darkness persisted. In the isbas, where even vermin starved, serfs cried for bread and died. In the schools, problems on the nature of angels' thoughts were anxiously discussed. In the streets, sudden cutthroats did for you and vanished. Yet one of them, Vanka Kaïn, the tsar of cutthroats, managed to be quite as surprising and infinitely more poetic than the anointed bandits with whom these pages deal. That is the grave inconvenience of history. In writing it, the historian may not sing the kings of the highroad. He must harp of the great carnivora. The bestiarium will reopen immediately.

For the people, in those days, existence was tragic. For the boiars it was gay. Shackled by Peter, they were halt. Under Elisabeth they could move. Provided they did not affront the imperial stare, they could live. In this epoch they began to. About them, from the toil of serfs, wealth had been accumulating. Splendidly they squandered it. In France, red-heeled seigneurs were similarly engaged. There, presently, the poor, bled to death to defray the follies of the rich, sent in their bill. History calls that bill the Terror. In Russia, the addition took longer. But when finally it was presented, the terror that resulted reduced that of France to the proportions of a farandole. It assembled all the terrors of tsardom and turned them upside down.

Muscovite follies began in the reign of this good Queen Bess. To encourage them, a great novelty had been introduced. The novelty was champagne. Other novelties followed: pineapples, Irish hunters, French literature, Italian music and the parage of princely display. When

a gentleman drove, two heiduques and ten lackeys accompanied him.   If he took snuff, he had
three hundred and sixty-five jewelled snuff-boxes
to choose from.   His coats were gorgeous and,
in the court of Elisabeth, his existence was Paph-
ian.

For the court, Elisabeth built the Winter Palace, the largest in Europe, precisely as Bucking-
ham is the ugliest and Versailles the least com-
fortable.

Versailles had other attributes.   In that El
Dorado of gallantry, vice was ennobled. Created
a marquis, it acquired a dignity ceremonial and
amusingly pompous.   Gallantry, which is the
parody of love, became its style and title.   Legitimate and royalist as the king, there was no
hypocrisy about it.   It was cynical but not perverse.   The perverse was there also, but hidden,
veiled by gold brocade, buried under fleurs-de-
lys.

The Winter Palace parodied Versailles as gallantry parodies love.   Lampsacene hymns, Lesbian songs, the rites of the gods of the cities that
mirrored their lunar towers in the Bitter Sea,
these, the ritual of halls that a league of candles
lit, made up in fervour what they lacked in grace.
The fault was Peter's who, without considering

the preliminary and very imperative educational steps, had ukased a social world into being.

The fault was not regarded as such. It was a sesame to the cave of forbidden fruit and resulted in a sans-gêne that no modern court has known, even behind the arras. As a consequence, the advent, elevation and passing of Elisabeth's grenadiers—lads of the moment they were called—young men lifted from the barracks to the couch of imperial amours, constituted a parade that was viewed with understanding, not with censure, except once. Two women presumed to sit in judgment. That was a serious matter. The beauty of one of the women exceeded Elisabeth's. That was more serious still. What followed is horrible.

The women were taken to the theatre. On the stage, one of them, the Countess Bestoujev, gave the executioner a handful of diamonds. The lash fell lightly on her back. The knife barely scratched her tongue. The other, the beauty, Countess Lapoukhin, screamed and fought with the man, bit his hand, resisted him as best she might. He tore her clothes off and, before applying the lash, cut her tongue out. Then, jeering at her nakedness, he offered the bloody morsel for a rouble. He turned to beat the beauty. She had fainted. The lash revived her. Pres-

ently for her and the other woman, the journey
to Siberia began.   Of all whom Elisabeth sent
there, these two only she neglected to recall.

In the private life of the nobles there were
incidents equally abominable. A woman of rank,
angered by a serf, got her fingers in his mouth
and tore it back to the ears.   In the bedroom of
another woman, a serf lived in a cage.   The
serf was a barber and the woman did not wish it
known that, when loosened, he dyed her hair.
Another woman, personally and unaided, killed
a hundred of her human chattels.   Another
woman—but here the pen balks.   Gautier said
that the inexpressible does not exist.   Gautier
did not live in eighteenth-century Russia.

In sending the Brunswickers to the devil,
Elisabeth directed them to the north, from
which, years later, they reached Denmark, minus
the boy tsar.   Ivan VI. was taken from them,
brought back, put in one prison, then in another,
though where and in what prison he never knew.
No one was allowed to tell him.   It was forbidden to speak to him.   To look at him was forbidden.   The Iron Mask of Russia, for twenty
years he reigned in an oubliette.   For crown, he
had cobwebs; for subjects, spiders; for kingdom,
a cell.

That grandeur was excessive.   It menaced

Elisabeth's. To annoy her, Frederick threatened to put him on the throne. "I'll chop his head off first," Elisabeth retorted. More finely, she nearly chopped Prussia's. In the interim she forgot Ivan. What she forgot, Catherine II. recalled. The Star of the North could not endure the rivalry even of a phantom. An attempt was made to rescue him. The keepers had their orders. The shadow tsar was killed.

That was Catherine's doing. Elisabeth objected to rivals also but not to shadows, only to women. With these she was merciless. Otherwise she enjoyed herself hugely. She hunted all day and danced all night. At some of the dances she appeared as a man. On such occasions it was etiquette for all court young women to appear as men and for all young men to appear as women. Elisabeth liked that. She liked young men in women's clothes. Moreover, that they might be properly sent out, she acted as dresser, selecting in the process those that pleased her most. In regard to her own masquerade she had a reason quite as interesting. Her leg was well turned, she knew she looked well as a man, knew, too, that women generally look the reverse. To be merely empress was insufficient. After the manner of a châtelaine in the days and in the lands of chivalry, she wanted to be Queen of Beauty and of Love.

In these diversions, age had the insolence to approach her. Illness dared to touch her. On her beauty they laid a smearing hand. That was crime, a crime long since codified—*crimen læsæ majestatis divinæ.*

The woman loved life, loved love, but she loved her beauty best. To it, to her gowns, her coiffure, her mirror, she gave contented hours. She never wore the same frock twice. No one was permitted to copy her coiffure until she had adopted another arrangement. One night she put a rose in her hair. The Countess Lapoukhin did the same. She got her face slapped for it, with the knout and Siberia to follow. As Elisabeth dealt it to that woman, the high fates dealt it to her. The knout was her mirror, her prison a darkened room. There, the goddess passed from sight, the sovereign disappeared. Like the countess, she was in the house of the dead.

There were hours when she meditated escape. The lustres were lighted and in a fresh Parisianism, her hair redressed, her face rerouged, her neck circled with emeralds as big and as naked as eggs, the illusion of lost beauty returned. But who was that rancid horror that stood and stared? From the mirror she turned, the illusion had gone and, weeping, she drank.

Her sins were scarlet. They might have been remitted if she had lived long enough. With longer life she would have washed them in the paler crimson of Frederick's blood. Her troops entered Berlin. East Prussia was theirs. Pommerania was theirs. Elisabeth directed them. More exactly, a thousand miles from the front, she shook her pen at her generals. "If any man wavers," that pen told Saltykov, "send him to me in chains."

They might have sent her the incompetent parvenu whom the lackeys of history call the Great, and who, serving as model for Wilhelm II., fled in fright from the battlefield as that fellow fled; bombarded cathedrals as he did under pretext that they served as conning towers; regarded treaties as the same scraps of paper; ordered the same frightfulness and pretended he had not; pretended also, precisely as that scrofulous dwarf pretended, that he did not want war and warred only because Europe was jealous. England, credulous as her lackeys, believed him. Just prior to Rossbach, he told d'Argens that, if he lost it, he would practise medicine. D'Argens nodded:—"Toujours assassin."

Elisabeth lacked the time to snuff him out but, for the remainder of the century, she snuffed

Prussia. That was the war-woman. The lady
of pleasure had other ideals. There was her
namesake, the first good Queen Bess. She
wanted to resemble her. She, too, wanted to parade as a Virgin Queen. The task was difficult,
but that made it all the more commendable.
Consequently, when she took it into her head to
marry, the ceremony was performed sub rosa.
The rose was not very tenebrous. The court,
Petersburg, everybody, even the dvorniks, looked
through it at the ceremony, which she had so
often omitted that it was thought highly original
of her to observe it at all.

The happy man was Russian. It is said that
she induced herself to accept him out of patriotism, in order that she and the throne might not
become the prey of some foreign prince. Everything is possible and it may be true. But the
compatriot whom she selected for her country's
sake, she had already selected for her own. He
was the tenor who preceded the regiment and,
though a tenor, not in the least ferocious, on the
contrary, an amiable, heavy-witted peasant in
Sunday clothes.

His name was Razoumovski. His father
kept a pothouse where his mother was waitress.
Good, plain, natural people, their son was the
proper mate for a servant-girl's daughter.

Known after the ceremony as the nocturnal emperor, his mother came to call. Suitably, or at all events ornamentally attired beforehand, she saw herself in a mirror, mistook what she saw for her daughter-in-law and fell on her knees.

The picture is Arcadian. To embellish it Razoumovski's behaviour was Boetian. He had none of Menchikov's pretensions, no Bühren ambitions, no Lynar airs. Years later, when Elisabeth was dead, he said that he had never been other than the most humble of her majesty's subjects. It was quite true. No jealousy of any kind. No interference of any sort. No views. The art of loving people as though you hated them was too complicated for this peasant who presented, in its perfection, a picture, life-size, of the mari sage, or rather would have, were it not that, like Amanda, he had one defect. He drank. But then the regiment that single file marched through the boudoir of his lady, any husband, however discreet, might wish to forget.

Drink aiding, he so thoroughly succeeded that, though made count, prince, field-marshal, his native simplicity remained unimpaired. Always and everywhere, in public, in private, in life and in death, he was the most humble of her majesty's subjects, except once, when, excited by liquor, he hit Saltykov over the head. What made the incident particularly awkward was Saltykov's inability to hit back. A nocturnal emperor was sacred. But that incident, the marriage itself, Razoumovski included, would not merit a footnote, were it not for a drama that ensued.

Paris, years later, became interested in a visitor of whom nothing was known and everything could be imagined. Young, fair, rich and mysterious, about her was the atmosphere of the faraway, a flavour that was heightened by her eyes which, like Ann Boleyn's, were of different colours. One was dark amber, the other deep blue. Her name, equally strange and oddly undulant, was Aly Emettée de Vlodomir, Princess Tarakanov.

What and where was Vlodomir? Who and what were the Tarakanovs? There was then no Almanach de Gotha to reply. But in the young woman's household there were those who did as well. Vlodomir and Tarakanov were domains of which their lady was lord. She may have been, but servants sometimes embroider.

Yet she had that air, remote, gracious, triste, which, in fairyland, poets and royals display. Estates, domains, patents of nobility, robes et manteaux, these things may be had. But that air, never! It is nowhere on sale. This girl exhaled it and, with it, the gift of the strange gods which innate charm is.

Whether she were or were not what she afterward claimed to be, is one of the minor enigmæ of history. But her belief in a secret that enveloped her, became the tragedy of her tragic life. On the sheer red peaks of torture, peaks that are the summits of human agony, she clung to it, refusing to retract, asking only that there be said over her a prayer for the dead.

In Paris, years ago, Flavinski, a Russian artist, exhibited a painting of which the horror and the execution detained. It showed this girl standing on a cot in a vault into which water poured through a grating. Her back against the wall, her head bent by the low roof, her hands clasped in terror, it was obvious that in a moment the water would reach and claim her.

The vault was a subterranean cell of a Petersburg prison which the Neva, rising, had flooded. Before Petersburg became Petrograd the cell was shown. Given the money and the guide and one can be shown anything. What the picture represented never occurred. The Princess Tarakanov was not drowned, she was murdered.

The story of the girl is brief, simple, bizarre and horrible. Her first memories were of a Rus-

sian convent from which, while still a child, she
was taken endlessly to Baghdad, thence on to
Isfahan, where she grew up in the palace of a
prince who treated her with a respect invariable
and profound.   Later she went with him to London.   There he left her, supplying her beforehand with money and an entourage and revealing to her a secret, of which long since whispers
had reached her, and concerning which docu-
mentary evidence would in time, he said, be produced.

It was in these circumstances that, vacating
London, she went to Paris, afterward to Vienna,
then to Venice, where the polite world was in-
trigued by this exotic princess who looked like a
houri and who lived like a vestal.

In that she reversed the order of things.   To
look like a vestal is always permissible, but to
live like one was not fashionable then.   At the
time, the fervours of Cyprus were forgotten.
The altars to Eros and Aphrodite were dust.
From the crystal parapets where they leaned
and laughed, the immortals had gone.   But not
very high, nor yet very far.   Over the eighteenth-
century metropoles of pleasure, they leaned and
laughed as before.   Their shrines had crumbled,
their temples had fallen, but their worship endured.   They were the immortals.   Modernity

could not touch them, time could not reach them, only their names had changed. Instead of Eros was Temptation; in place of Aphrodite, Delight. In the current literature were their rituals; in paintings and statues, their images; in opera, their hymns. The contagion of their rites fevered and depraved.

In the amorality of the neo-pagan atmosphere, the princess really loved. She loved in an epoch when no one loved at all. It was very eccentric of her. To be eccentric is always hazardous. The danger was there. She mistook it for bliss. In that disguise it caught and killed her.

A prince asked her hand. The prince was Radziwill, a Polish refugee, who travelled about with the twelve apostles, life-size, in massive gold, which, in accordance with his needs, he melted.

In considering the proposal, which she presently rejected, she told him the secret. It was so inspiring that with it he planned to have the Sultan put them both on the throne of the Jagellons. Whether he were suited for it is unimportant. But she looked the queen which she might have been, though not perhaps in Poland. Apparently, too, the time had come. From Isfahan the other prince, the Persian, sent her the promised papers.

Among them was Elisabeth's will. Elisabeth then was dead. Catherine II. had succeeded her. According to the documents, the accession was illegal. In the will, Elisabeth appointed her daughter to succeed her and that daughter, issue of her marriage with Razoumovski, was Aly Emettée de Vlodomir.

At the time, she was in the ideal city of the material world. Venice should have detained this girl who embodied its charm. But the dream that always had been with her and which, it may be, had given her the look, enigmatically triste, which they alone display whom destiny has marked for some fate, supreme or tragic, that dream, or that destiny, held her and led her and hid her away.

Then, too, a rumour of the will, the report that she was granddaughter of Peter the Great, the evocation of power absolute, these things and her presence, sovereign, gracious, sad, stirred Venice. Along the liquid streets ran the ripple of the cry, *"Viva l'imperatrice!"*

That also may have been coercive. Presently, in addition, there was love.

Radziwill, meanwhile, more enthusiastic, more enamoured and more absurd than ever, melted his last apostle. Clearly the Sultan, Perfume of Paradise, Shadow of God on Earth, could refuse nothing to a descendant of the Porte's arch-foe. The plan was magnificent, it was also insane. The princess, disassociating herself from him and from it, went to Ragusa, where she sent the admiral of a Russian squadron, then at Leghorn, a copy of her mother's will.

The admiral, Alexis Orlov, had been Catherine's lover. He referred the matter to her. In reply he was commanded to seize the claimant at any cost, even though he had to bombard the coast to get her.

That order, if executed, meant war. It is perhaps obvious that Catherine, in giving it, knew the facts and preferred war to their recognition.

Historians generally have ignored that point. Generally they have ignored the princess. Otherwise they have derided her. To some, her Persian was a fabulous being. To others, her purity was as mythical. Challemel-Lacour described her as an adventuress. She may have been. But some time later, de Verac, the French minister at Petersburg, received a bill which he was asked to collect. The bill was from a Paris merchant who claimed that the Princess Tarakanov owed him fifty thousand francs. De Verac had never heard of the lady. At headquarters he asked about her. He was requested not to ask again, but he was told that the bill would be paid, which it was, although bills incurred by the Russian squadron in French waters were protested and payment refused. Privately, his enquiries continued. From the secret service he learned that the princess was Elisabeth II.

In those days communication was very leisurely. When Orlov received Catherine's commands, the course he adopted was characteristically that of the average Russian of whom it is characteristic not to have any character at all. He prostrated himself before the girl whom he called his empress and to whom he swore the fealty of a knight. The sad girl listened, listened longer, listened as she had listened to no man before. Orlov was a giant and an athlete. Because of a fight in which he had sunk the Turkish fleet, he was called a hero. He looked it. He was superiorly handsome. Though a ruffian, he, too, could charm. That charm encircled her. Italy and youth and love! Love in the land where, said Owen Meredith, "love most lovely seems!"

In the girl's entourage there were those who doubted, who warned, who perhaps foresaw. But the girl who had never yet loved, then loved wholly. The man, his splendid vigour, his knightly allegiance, enthralled. Then too there was the dream into which he entered with her. He told her, what was true, that he and his brothers had put Catherine on the throne. He added, what was false, that he and his brothers would take it from her. Then, if his lady but deigned, she and he could share it.

In the passionate wooing the impassioned girl was won. She became his wife and, amid the boom of guns and acclaiming cries, went with him to the flagship, where instantly he disappeared. About her were marines. She was a prisoner. A prisoner she remained until she reached Petersburg where Catherine had her put to the question, tortured to death.

The throne then was secure. From it Catherine had torn an emperor whom she murdered. From it she had held another emperor whom she killed. There were no more claimants. The last of the Romanovs was dead, and at her latest lover the empress leered.

VENUS VICTRIX

FROM the cupboard of yawns that history is, Catherine the Greater emerges in spangles. Her life was an opera composed by Chance. Musicians do not know him; mythographers do not mention him, mathematicians deny that he is. Yet, drawn in a chariot of jewels by horses of flame, those whom he favours are raised to the sky. Chance carried her portrait from a tinpot principality to the great Peter's grandson and herself to the throne.

That grandson, a poodle-faced boy, pock-marked, witless, neurotically unable to be still, and whose tongue, when not wagging with inanities, hung like a hound's from his mouth, was the son of the Duchess of Holstein-Gottorp, Elisabeth's sister. Appointed tsarevitch, he was given for bride the Princess Sophia Augusta of Anhalt-Zerbst, whom the Church christened Catherine; and Voltaire, Semiramis.

The name rolls; it is empty as sound. Semiramis never existed. But the name subsists. It means the One who Loves. As such it fitted this girl who was to become the grande amoureuse and whose dramatic entrance into history was effected with a swoon. At sight of the whelp she fainted.

A virgin and—in appearance—very ethereal, she had two ambitions. She wanted the mantle of glory. She wanted the perfume of Eros. She wanted to be Venus Victrix.

At the time, a Psyche on a fan, slight and very fair, her mouth was red as sealing-wax, her hair an auburn turban. Her eyes, sometimes heliotrope, were sometimes green, sometimes grey. In later years, dignity replaced the deliciousness that had been. In lieu of Psyche, there was Juno. With age came the sibyl, a sybil obese, dropsical, sinister. But when she left Stettin, where she had played with ragamuffins in the sullen streets, and journeyed to Russia and the throne, it was endearing to see the blushes, the ingenuousness, the modesty that she displayed. She looked precisely what she was, fresh from school, pretty enough to eat— while preparing to devour an empire.

In her memoirs she says that already she had determined to have it and have it alone. By way of preparation for the meal, she sharpened her teeth on Machiavelli, taught herself Russian and meditated the mosaics of the Greek faith. In marrying the whelp that faith would have to be hers. But she had no inconvenient scruples. She would have become Mormon if necessary and though it was not, she did. That, though, was later. Meanwhile, from the swoon into which the prospective delights of marriage with the poodle-faced boy had thrown her, she got herself together, got the whelp and, when the throne was his, put him from it as a child is put to sleep. For soothing syrup he had poison; for lullaby, contempt; for cradle, a grave.

The whelp—historically Peter III.—was a German. He was born a German, died a German. Frederick, at the time, was on his knees. This imbecile first raised him up, then knelt before him. From that day, Prussia began an ascent that culminated at the Marne. The original Romanov was a Prussian. Peter III. was a Hun.

Among other children of Catherine was Paul, who succeeded her. In her memoirs she says that Peter the Little was not Paul's father. Historians who know more about it than she did, insist that he was. In listening to them, one might mistake the lady for an austere matron. The error would have annoyed her. She had no false pride. On the other hand, she did have a few lovers. Among them was Saltykov, who may have been Paul's father. But, as Voltaire said, and said too very reasonably:—"These are family matters."

All that was later. At the start, Catherine, who had determined to be first, began by being last. Before commanding, she obeyed; before usurping, she effaced herself. To Elisabeth, she was adorably subservient; to Peter, unutterably considerate; to the court—amazed at such guile-lessness—she was delightfully ingénue. To no one, however obscure, was she negligent. She importuned no one, however great. She gave everything and asked nothing. The rose was her model. She charmed and was silent. Yet, without seeming to listen, she heard everything. Apparently ethereal, she was preparing to gobble a throne.

Hunger appeased, Cinderbritch vanished. The swooning virgin had gone. To the court's astonishment, an ingénue became a general; a girl, a despot. Peter the Great made Russia recognise Europe. Catherine the Greater made Russia recognised by the world. That is history. When enemies were arming, concerning their number she never enquired. What she asked was:—"Where are they?" That is Ro-

CATHERINE II

man. When she learned that Diderot was poor, she bought his library, made him its custodian and paid him a salary for fifteen years in advance. That is delightful. When her purse was empty she evoked the ghost of gold that paper money is and saddled her country with debt. Had she wished she could have manufactured money out of leather, out of blades of grass and given it any value she liked. She could do anything and did almost everything. She cowered but once. That was at the sight of the French revolution. Immediately she straightened. Her little household, as she called Russia, was not France. Moreover, she commanded an army that fought without pay, without rest, often without food and always without complaint. Against that army no revolution could prevail. No, nor Asia either. Had she lived, she would have owned it.

Beside her, Peter, her lord, looked exactly what he was and nothing worse can be said of him—an imbecile who drilled tin soldiers, dressed wax dolls, trained terriers in his bedroom, occupied his absence of mind with grotesque puerilities, worshipped Frederick, made peace with Prussia, prussianised the army, got drunk with his lackeys and foisted on the court a band of Holsteiners as ignoble—if that be possible—as himself. Catherine, meanwhile, belle comme le jour, to employ her own description of herself, was dreaming of grandeur absolute. By way of practise, she managed the idiot's duchy. Later, when the dream came true, she found it quite as easy to manage his empire. She was a born administrator and yet a woman. But what a woman! Cæsar and Faustine combined.

Faustine had many lovers. Catherine had more. But before she was empress only a few, just enough to hand her up on the throne from which they pulled her husband off. In tsaral annals, the modus of the elimination, then unique, was to become common. Peter III. was murdered. He was given arsenic in vodka. The poison being ineffective, Alexis Orlov knocked him down, held him down and strangled him with a napkin. Orlov's punishment, highly dramatic, and equally delayed, will be told later on. For the murder itself, Catherine has been rebuked. Perhaps it had its excuse. Prior to Elisabeth's death, Peter the Small had made it clear to Semiramis that once tsar he would divorce and replace her, as Peter the Great's wife had been replaced, by a scullion. Catherine had therefore the choice between immolating and being immolated. It was at dinner that she decided.

Tacitus tells of a supper, given by Nero to Britannicus, who died of it. "After a moment of silence," the historian noted, "gaiety returned." *Post breve silentium, repetitia convivii lætitia.* The dinner resembled that supper.

The dinner was held in a high hall, hung with Asiatic splendour, flooded with European light. The foreign ministers were there, the great nobles, the ladies of honour, a swarm of princes and peris perfumed with lies, starred with diamonds, radiant as rainbows.

Peter, rising, proposed the health of the imperial family. Catherine remained seated. Why not? The imperial family consisted of herself; of Paul, who was a child; of Peter, who was her husband.

"Doura!" Peter the Small bawled at her. "Fool!"

Everybody heard, except Catherine. With a smile she turned to one of her gentlemen. With a fresher smile she turned to another. A moment merely. But in that moment a grave had been dug. Then she looked at Peter. So must Nero have looked at Britannicus.

Peter counted for little. What he did count for was German. Petersburg had an indigestion of Teuton customs, Teuton manners, Teuton touts. Catherine was not Teuton. She had begun by being German but the taint had been drained. She had become wholly Russian prior to becoming entirely French. The versatility of her universality enthralled prelates and pretorians, the boiars and the army. When the time came, she but lifted her finger. They rose to her.

The dinner was in celebration of peace with Prussia whom Elisabeth, had she lived, would have knifed. A few days later, Peter celebrated the peace again, but on this occasion at Oranienbaum, a plaisance where Catherine omitted to accompany him.

Incidentally the Orlovs were at work, five of them, five brothers, five men with one head, each of whom commanded a regiment, in one of which Potemkin was lieutenant. Gregori Orlov, the eldest of the brothers, but though the eldest still very young, had so charmed Catherine that familiarly she was called Madame Gregori. He was one of the men to whom she had turned and smiled on the night of the dinner. The other man was Alexis Orlov, who had charmed her also.

Early one morning, shortly after, Alexis Orlov brought her, dressed as a general, to the barracks. There, a priest, raising a cross, recited an oath. The soldiers repeated it. A cry went up, "Live the empress!" In that cry Petersburg joined.

To the blare of brass, the regiments started, Catherine on horseback leading. Peter got wind of it. He fled to a fortress. The wind had preceded him.

From a rampart a sentry called:—"Who goes there?"

"The emperor."

"There is no emperor. Move on!"

Peter turned and, whimpering like a beaten cur, offered to share the sceptre. Catherine declined. He begged for mercy. Officially, his death was ascribed to apoplexy. Crétinism were more exact.

Peter had many defects. The gravest was an inability to appreciate a Tiberius in skirts. That fault official Russia did not share. It rose to her and it knelt. Then, presently, about the throne, the perfume of Eros mounted.

In the ballroom of her heart, the Orlovs were not her first partners, nor were they the last. Their predecessors were not numerous, but their successors were without number. Moralists have blamed her for that and no doubt very justly. None the less, her cotillon favours represented something else than the caprices of an empress autocratically privileged to do as she liked. Catherine elevated her men Pompadours to the dignity of a state institution. They had appointments, prerogatives, and a position that was exceeded only by her own and which frequently was on an equality with it. Several offended her greatly, successively she wearied of each, yet to all she was decent, none incurred her dislike. One, whom she surprised with her nearest friend, she dismissed, but not to Siberia. Another she relinquished to a rival, without chopping his head off first. Christine of Sweden had a faithless du Barry killed in her presence. Queen Elisabeth was as bloody. Lovers of whom Catherine wearied or who wearied of her, preserved her friendship, enjoyed her protection. When their intimacy with her ended, their service to the state began. Or, if they lacked the ability, they lived semi-royally on her royal largesse.

The first to gather her handkerchief was Saltykov, a young assembly of brilliant vices whose assiduities, favoured for reasons dynastic, were interrupted. He was given an honorific exile and sent as minister to Sweden. Catherine, who was not then Semiramis, but grand-duchess merely, shed no tears. The lustre of his bril-

liance had been already dimmed. Into her ken
another partner had swum. The new planet
was Poniatowski, a tourist from Poland who
returned there as king.

The kingship had been predicted. When but
a child an astrologer drew his horoscope. In
it was a throne. What throne? Nobody knew,
but he was trained for it as a colt is trained for
a race. In the training he acquired the attitude and strut of a king on the stage. That was
mere façade. Back of it was the ingenuousness
of a young lady, and fronting it was a smile in
which there was Château Yquem. Such a smile
is heady. It captivated Catherine. But though
he had a languorous eye on her, he had another
and a very timorous one on Siberia. In Russia,
one never knew! Besides, he barely escaped it.

Late one night he reached the grand-ducal
residence where Catherine awaited him. While
effecting a surreptitious entrance, he was surprised by the guard and taken to Peter. At
the moment, the future monarch was guzzling
with his lady, a very elegant young person,
squint-eyed, stupid, malodorous, who, Masson
says, spat when she talked.

Peter grinned. "Come to assassinate me?"

Poniatowski, his façade crumbling, stam-
mered a protest.

Peter giggled. "He, he! You're after the grand-duchess. Well, run along. I, too, have a girl."

Subsequently, Catherine gave him a crown. That bit of jewellry was his walking-stick. She made him king to be rid of him. Poland, the mad nation, a nation chivalrous, heroic, insane, removed it. Poland that had withstood the Tatars and was to withstand everything, could not stand a young lady, though recently she listened to a pianist. From the Slav Valhalla, with what fierce surprise, the Jagellons, her warrior kings, must have looked down at that!

Catherine's handkerchief passed from Poniatowski to the Orlovs, from them to Potemkin, from him to Zubov. Saltykov and Poniatowski were her maîtres de danse. In the great cotillon that followed, the Orlovs mark the beginning, Potemkin the height, Zubov the end. Intermediately were other partners, though how many, history, her hostess, fatigued by the task of enumerating them, neglected to count. But in the long bacchanal, Gregori Orlov detained her most.

Vigorous, violent, fearless, a giant in stature, Gregori Orlov was the handsomest man of his day. After the manner of giants he was dull. But he looked every inch the sultan that he became. He not only looked the sultan, he filled the rôle. To him, Semiramis was but another odalisque in the seraglio which he maintained. Catherine tolerated his impertinences, ignored his infidelities, forgave whatever he did. Catherine loved him. More exactly, like every grande amoureuse, and of them all she was the greatest, when she said je t'aime she meant je m'aime and failed to see the difference. Nor did Orlov see it. He thought of marrying her. It seemed the simplest thing in the world. She had given him honours, titles, palaces, serfs by the thousand, domains by the league. She shared the treasury with him. But the throne, no. There pride interfered, the consciousness that however she might condescend, the sceptre must remain indivisibly hers. Then also, while Orlov had practically put the sceptre in her hand, while, too, he was a sort of Greek god, yet the coup d'état had been to him merely an adventure, and his divinity was of the early and very primitive type. The god was null. Presently the nullity was revealed. To have an empress at his feet was insufficient. He ran off with a chit of a girl, who died, and the pulp behind his forehead deglutinised. He went mad, covering his face with offal which, like Ezechiel, he ate.

At the time, the madness was said to have been caused not at all by grief, but by an herb with which Potemkin poisoned him.

Potemkin too was mad, not from an herb, but with genius. One of the many who handed Catherine up on the throne, he began, on the morning of the coup d'état, by offering her a silver feather for her uniform and might have ended by putting the Byzantine crown on her head. On the morning of the revolution, he was an ensign. Orlov gone, he was vice-emperor. Between those sentences there are years. There is also an ascent from nowhere to everything. Catherine made him prince, premier, plutocrat, generalissimo. With the Crimea and the Black Sea, royally he repaid her.

Women admire the brave but they prefer the audacious. Saltykov was a ladies' man. Poniatowski was a lady. Orlov was a devil, Potemkin was a demon. The cotillon which Catherine danced with these and with other men and in which she displayed a temperamental intemperance more extravagant than any that the modern world has beheld, represents the spaciousness of her heart, which many entered and none could fill. Saltykov surprised her. Poniatowski charmed her. Orlov carried her off her feet. Potemkin held her in the air. Her interest in

Saltykov and in Poniatowski was that of the amateur in experimental physiology. But it was Orlov who taught her to love and Potemkin who taught her to reign. If neither became her master, it was because no man could be that.

Potemkin was also a giant, a giant with one eye. In a tavern brawl he had lost the other. Alexis Orlov knocked it out. Gregori Orlov was gigantic and violent. Alexis Orlov was gigantic and brutal. Potemkin was gigantic and terrible. A dark cyclops with the air of a jackal and the negligences of a pasha, he was the only one of Catherine's partners whom she had not selected for his looks, but also he was the only one who spared her the advances which she was always obliged to make, the only one who dared. That won her to this man, who loved her with the tenderness of an amant and the poetry of a troubadour. She was his mistress and his glory. When satiety came, ambition linked them still.

Incidentally, she was pushing the frontiers back, extending her little household, at the north, to the aurora; at the east to the dawn; at the south, nearly to the gates of Stamboul.

In the extension, Potemkin greatly aided. To her ménage he added the Crimea and then took her to see it.

It would have been interesting to have accompanied her in the Arabian Night entertainment that he devised and through which in a
sleigh—Cleopatra's barge on runners and for
which, and for her suite that followed, there
were five hundred horses at each relay—she
passed down from polar ice to a tropical sun,
from Petersburg to the Euxine, from surprise
to enchantment, from the emptied thrones of Tatar khans to the abandoned divans of Ottoman
viceroys, from fallen palaces of kings of the
Bosphorus to the crumbled temples of Hercules
and Diana, from memories of Mithridates to
the myths of Greece, from illusion to illusion,
through scenery painted on canvas, through pan-
oramas that vanished as she passed, through
trained ballets of acclaiming crowds, through
cascading fireworks, through uninterrupted
fêtes, down into glowing gardens where Walla-
chian hospodars, Circassian princes, dispossessed
Georgian lords genuflected to the Star of the
North, who, at the end of the route, saw a tri-
umphal arch on which blazed an inscription—
"The Way to Stamboul."

At one halt, Catherine was greeted by the
Austrian emperor, disguised as a gentleman; at
another by Poniatowski, disguised as a king.

Ségur—French minister to the court of Semiramis—who went with her, said that the meeting between the ex-amants was formal. What did he expect? But presently the two retired into privacy where they probably talked of old times as old people do. On emerging, Poniatowski had mislaid his hat. Catherine found and restored it.

"Ah!" said Poniatowski with his Château Yquem smile. "You gave me once a far finer one."

Ségur said that Catherine's conversation was very banal. Poniatowski may have copied it.

Near Moscow, on the return flight, an opera was given in the private theatre of a resident count. The composer, the librettist, the singers, the musicians, the corps de ballet, everybody connected with the representation—except the count's guests—were his serfs. Earlier that day the tenor, who took the part of a king, had been flogged. At a supper which followed, Ségur noted that the goblets, enough for a hundred, were incrusted with jewels.

Potemkin surpassed the count. In magnificence, he exceeded Catherine. His entertainments bewilder the pen. The paragraphs that tell of them dazzle. The Crimean junket, the unequalled journey through the antique Taurida, was but one of the many flowers that he put at his sovereign's feet. At a ball which he gave for her, lackeys handed about goblets filled with diamonds to the brim.

– Hero and lover, doubly triumphant, he too thought of marrying his queen. It seemed to him, as it had seemed to Orlov, the simplest thing in the world. Catherine regarded the matter as before. He threatened to become a monk. For a cyclops and a jackal, the threat was ridiculous. Catherine laughed. The charm was broken. Friendship remained. Potemkin, fantastic in all things, demonstrated his in a manner that was perhaps original. He made lists of eligible young men and, with the lists, submitted their portraits. It was for Catherine to choose. For a while, she did. But Zubov, who succeeded them all, she selected unassisted.

Saltykov entered her life when she was young, Zubov when she was old. Young she was delicious. Age moldered her. Seen across a room she was still imperial. Close to, was a toothless woman with furtive eyes, a quavering voice and passions still unappeased. Yet, far or near, her power was predominant. The splendour of her court, the pomp of her princes, the extent of her dominions, created an admiration that was stupefying. Her prestige surpassed the forgotten glories of Louis XIV. But in the same manner that her fame transcended his, her bacchanals exceeded Faustine's. There are planes beneath which there is perhaps nothing deeper. Tiberius devised vices for which names had to be coined. The Winter Palace became a Tiberian villa. Zubov, young enough to be her grandson, had companions in arms, and in his and in their company, while her troops beat the Turks, fought the Swedes, devastated Poland, the sinister and prodigious woman achieved the ultimate descent.

Zubov's portrait was not submitted by Potemkin, it was self-presented. He put himself where Catherine could see him. Any officer who had, or who thought he had, a well-turned leg did the same. The state apartments were lined with fetching young men. They formed a hedge along which the sovereign passed, looked, smiled, passed on. Zubov followed the smile. It led him far and high. Another subaltern was a fille entretenue. With none of Orlov's dash, without a spark of Potemkin's ability, he obtained from her more power than either, more wealth than both. In the last years of her reign, Zubov was automatically and autocratically tsar.

His portrait, which Potemkin neglected, Masson displayed. It shows a youth in a dressing-gown and not a very decent one, waited on by his valets, the lords and princes of the realm. His back is turned. But in a mirror before him, his face appears, cold, vain, empty. In his hand is a book; on his shoulder a monkey. Meanwhile his valets stand and wait, wait and stand until he deigns to turn, deigns to look. At that condescension, instantly they prostrated themselves before the Pompadour who had been emptying the treasury, filling the prisons and whom no one, unpermitted, dared to address. There were those who were there on matters of state. Day in, day out, month after month they came before the permission was accorded. Then negligently, in that negligée, the tsar dismissed them.

Slight of body and slimmer of soul, he may have possessed, Masson, for finishing touch, concludes, occult qualities which only Catherine could appreciate. No doubt. Besides, to the old woman that she was, he was spring, fair skies, youth's return and she a girl again, loved as Poniatowski had loved her, for her charm alone. There is sorcery in that and in the first enthrallment of it she regarded him as a genius. Afterward she saw him more after the manner of a sultana on whose neck is a eunuch's heel.

Potemkin, at the time, was at Jassy. He

started for Petersburg. On a highway he died. It was reported that Zubov had had him poisoned. Perhaps he had. But an annalist says that during a fever that overtook him en route, he ate a whole ham, a smoked goose, three chickens, drank liquor by the quart, drenching himself alternately with ice-water and cologne. Gigantic and fantastic in life, fantastically and gigantically he died. At the news of it, the sultana leered at the eunuch.

Zubov is the smear on the chronicles of a woman sovereignly enabled to do as she liked and who was very polite about it. One after another she killed the last three Romanovs and ran Poland through the heart. To-day, these things are forgotten. The blood has dried, only dust remains and the fading memory of an empress whose life was a decameron to be read with pursed lips. But in her were Alexandrine ambitions. The route which Potemkin blazed the way, she would have followed to St. Sophia and beyond it to Delhi and the peacock throne. She had the will, the ability, the power. What she lacked was time. Apoplexy battened on her as she had on Warsaw. It is said that she gave up the ghost with a shriek. Was it Poland that she saw?

Indulgent and cruel, prodigal and mean, a

woman in whom every contradiction was resumed, Catherine was an empress who made enormous an empire already vast; a tsaritsa who enumerated her victories and could not count her amours; a conqueror who had Adonis for secretary of the treasury and Apollo for minister of war; a cynic who slaughtered Poland and called herself a pupil of Voltaire; a sovereign before whom the entire pageant of passion and glory unrolled; a tyrant and a lesbian who passed through history dripping with blood and exhaling the perfume of Eros.

Succinctly, a great temperament; concisely, a great man; summarily, the least detestable despot of the lot, and yet, primarily, a German girl who had come to Russia without a penny and without a friend.

Shortly after she reached Petersburg her father died. He died on his barren farm, which was called a principality.

"It is ridiculous of you to cry," Elisabeth told her. "You ought to know better. Your father was nobody."

Elisabeth was too civil to add "and a pauper." Besides, as she perhaps divined, the girl was superiorly endowed. Catherine had assets. The assets were appetites. She gorged them. During a reign that lasted from the middle of the

eighteenth century to the beginning of the nineteenth, an empty-handed nobody gave her lovers
the equivalent of half a billion and ruled fifty
different races with a despotism that was identical for each.

Previously Psyche, she was Venus Victrix
then. At her feet lay all the Russias. To her
the whole of Europe bowed. At her left was
a son whom she hated; at her right a lover whom
she paid. Seated between them on the tallest
of earthly thrones, covered and crowned with
diamonds and with gold, she knew, as no other
woman has known, how love and glory taste.
The bitterness of them filled her toothless mouth.

VII

PAUL

CATHERINE, who entered history with a swoon, departed with a shriek. At the shriek, Night unfurled her great black fan. Another reign of terror had begun. The shriek proclaimed Paul emperor. The proclamation was involuntary. Catherine did not want Paul to rule. She had arranged otherwise. He ruled, none the less, and in such a manner that at his own exit he also shrieked. With that shriek for motif, Bovery composed an opera, and Petersburg a Te Deum.

Paul's coronation robe should have been a straitjacket. Ivan was mad. Peter was mad. Their madness appals, but it fascinates. In horror raised to the ultimate degree there is grandeur. Paul's insanity took the form of microphilia. Domitian was a microphile. He specialised in flies. Heliogabalus was a microphile. He collected cobwebs. Microphilia is the insanity of the petty.

The maladies and particularly the deaths of

those emperors should have instructed Paul.
Besides, since their day, times had changed.
They had changed, too, since the days of Ivan
and of Peter. Catherine's reign had been a liberal education. She scandalised Europe, murdered her husband, killed Peter's nephew, crucified Elisabeth's daughter, slaughtered Prague,
assassinated Warsaw, destroyed Poland and
hated her son. She was a well-bred woman. But
men no longer had their heads chopped off for
a yes or a no. Women's tongues might wag,
they were not torn out for that reason. Catherine was indulgent. Paul was modest.

"I will thank you to understand," he told an
envoy who had spoken of some boiar as an important person, "that there is but one important
person in Russia. That is the person whom I
happen to address and his importance lasts only
while I am addressing him."

The microphile was a megalomaniac. That
was not his mother's fault. Catherine dwarfed
and hated him, as she hated and dwarfed her
husband. The hatred that she had for her son
is the sole evidence that he was legitimate.
Psychologically, the evidence had its weight.

Paul examined it and turned to Poniatowski.
"Are you my father?"

The problem was delicate, the solution ob-

scure. Poniatowski, who was then old, fat, rheu-
matic and a king no longer, shook his head and
sat down.

With imperial brevity, Paul again addressed
him. "Stand!"

He turned anew to the evidence. It seemed con-
clusive. He gave orders accordingly. The orders, spectacular in their theatrical effect, will
be recited in a moment.

When Catherine shrieked, Paul was married,
middle-aged, the father of three sons, two of
whom successively succeeded him. The shriek
reached him at Gatchina, a country fortress near
Petersburg, where he lived with a Würtemburg
woman, who was his wife; with an embittered
young Russian, who was the dearer one yet, and
with a regiment which he dressed and drilled,
Prussian fashion, whip in hand. The fashion
was otherwise observed. The uniform was Prussian, but one that Prussia had long since abandoned. Paul loved it. He loved the past. Except such torture as he could inflict, it was the
only thing that he did love.

The atmosphere of Gatchina was grand-ducal,
pestilential and penitentiary. Travellers avoided
it. Above, in a turret, was a telescope. There
Paul sat. Any one whom he could spy afar
making a détour to keep out of his way, he sent

cavalry to overtake and imprison. "Let me be hated," said Caligula. "But let me be feared."

Paul was Caligula in miniature. Like him, he was hideous but, excessive in every form of hideousnesss, he was more hideous. He had the face of a cat, a dead cat, a dead Kalmuck skunk, and with that death's-head on a short pudgy body, he strutted. After Catherine's exit, he strutted crowned. In his palaces, he was the monarch that the old pictures show. On parade, he was the drill-sergeant, but everywhere the bully. In behalf of some one, Alexander, his son, at the time but a boy, fell at his feet, begged him to be merciful. Paul kicked him in the face.

"Sacha, was it you who killed him?" that boy's mother afterward asked.

At Gatchina, he spied a giant on horseback racing toward the fortress. The giant was Nikolai Zubov, brother of the Pompadour en titre. The shock of the sight of him gave Paul the colic. He thought he had come to arrest him. Zubov had been hastening to announce that Catherine was in extremis. The colic passed, but another fear gripped him. To allay it, off he rode.

At the Winter Palace, Catherine was unconscious. Up the great stairway, through a double

hedge of Circassians, and on through high halls
filled with courtiers and lackeys, Paul passed to
her apartments.   Before he reached them, the
death-rattle had begun.

In one room was an escritoire and near it
an open fire.   Paul opened the desk.   Among
the papers was an order for his arrest.   He gave
it to the flames.   Another paper was a will in
which his mother appointed his son, Alexander,
her successor.   That also he destroyed.

He turned.   Before him was the Pompadour.
Behind Zubov was a throng of nobles.   Paul
lifted his dead-cat face.   With a pudgy hand
he gestured.

"I am your emperor!"

Instantly Zubov, to whom all Russia cringed,
was cringing.   Instantly the nobles were on their
knees.

It was then that Night unfurled her great
black fan.   A reign of terror had begun.

The old courtesan that history is, had her attenuations for Paul, as she had her myopia for
Ivan, her cecity for Peter.   An age-long supper
on abominations made her indulgent.   Youth
is always intolerant.   Tacitus branded, Juvenal
flayed.   History then was a débutante.   To-day
she candies her tales, throws orange blossoms
on the tomb of Lucrezia Borgia and immortelles

PAUL I

on Paul's. Beneath the weeds, Paul has the faded air of a noble character thwarted and misunderstood. But pulled down a chimney by his bandy legs and run through for his crimes? Nowhere in Russian history is that recorded. History is the one book that has no end.

Sixty years later, a boy, afterward Alexander III., told a comrade that he had discovered a state secret—the Emperor Paul was assassinated!

Among the attenuations put on Paul's tomb was his grand-ducal existence. Catherine made it a long humiliation. A man who is a man rises from an insult refreshed. It is perhaps a tonic. In a microphile it secretes venom, of which the chemical precipitate is spite. When Catherine's crown passed to Paul he spat on it and ordered another.

Masson, an idler in Petersburg, says that in the processions of peoples, the ark of the covenant was not surrounded by greater pomp than was that new crown during its journey from the jeweller's to the palace. At the palace, the jeweller-Pygmalion was compelled to kneel in worship to it.

It was in that crown that the misunderstood lunatic strutted. Always a comic figure—at a safe distance—his mother made him ridiculous.

While lovers of hers, who were younger than his sons, governed Russia and waded in gold, he was put on an allowance, put in a corner, treated as nobody. Night after night, he and his sons with him, had seen her dismiss the court and march off with some Pompadour who always ignored them. For less than that, Catherine had put her husband in the grave. Paul could have put her in the street. It was not natural affection or filial respect that restrained him. He loathed her as completely as she abominated him. But Catherine, with all her faults, with all her sins, and all her crimes, was brave. Paul, a born bully and, for that reason, a born coward, was afraid of her. With her husband, with Ivan VI. and Elisabeth's daughter for examples, he had cause. He was not a match for her.

He was not a match for anyone. Since Pultowa, everywhere the Russian arms were victorious. During Paul's reign, generally they were defeated.

Immortelles, however plentiful, cannot alter that. None the less the circumstances of his pre-monarchal career may have prepared him to be what he became, a tyrant, conceited, fantastic, implacable, mad as a hatter, his pockets stuffed with ukases about nothing at all. To say as much, or rather as little, was impossible. In holy

Russia, a tsar was sacrosanct, an abyss of knowl-
edge, a star of truth. It was quite in that light
that Paul regarded himself. All lunatics are
imaginative. With power added, sometimes
they are spectacular. It is then that they become interesting.

Catherine's body was embalmed and put on a
great bed in the throne-room. The embalming,
very artistically effected, made her black and
orange. People who had beheld her in her
splendour, marvelled then at her hideousness.
They did not realise that for the first time they
saw her as she really was.

Beside her, on that bed, Paul put another
corpse. The watchman whom he selected to
stand guard at night was Alexis Orlov. Catherine's bedfellow was her husband's skeleton. It
was Alexis Orlov who had killed him. In the
vast room, which candles feebly lit, Orlov's vigil
must have been Dantesque. But the ghosts of
that couple, surprised enough to find themselves
again together, what spectral secrets they must
have muttered, not only to each other, but at
him!

The scene, thoroughly Æschylean, was succeeded by another that did not surpass it, perhaps nothing could, but which Hugo should
have painted. During the funeral that followed,

Orlov was compelled to walk, carrying the crown he had wrenched from Peter the Little, and to walk directly behind the coffin into which he had strangled him. Such stagecraft deserves applause.

From the funeral, Paul turned to affairs of state. Catherine's reign had been a golden age. The massacres committed by her indemnified those who had missed the butcheries of anterior tsars. But the beautiful custom of throwing yourself from your conveyance and grovelling in the snow, in the mud, to the sovereign that passed, Semiramis abolished. With a ukase, Paul revived it.

Presently, a woman drove by. She had not heard of the ukase. She had never seen Paul. She lived in the country. There, her husband was dying. She was hurrying for a physician. She did not notice a madman on horseback. She was thinking of her husband, of the physician who might save him. On she drove.

Paul, twisting in the saddle, motioned. "Arrest her!"

Explanations, excuses, prayers, tears, these things availed her nothing. Afar her husband waited, wondered, hoped, despaired, agonised and died. In the stone sack where she was

thrown, mercifully a fever came in which she
joined him.

Paul dealt with the army as he dealt with
that woman. For the slightest inadvertence, arrest. Generals came to the daily drill with travelling bags. They never knew at what moment
or for what reason Paul would order them seized
and carted away. On one occasion a line wavered. "Halt!" Paul ordered. "March!" he continued and added:—"To Siberia!"

Discipline first, accoutrements next. Since
Peter's day, the uniform of the Russian soldier
had been warm without being heavy, easy without being loose. Paul trussed the troops in a
uniform so tight that if a soldier fell he could
barely rise unassisted. On one occasion a horse
stumbled. Paul had the animal starved to death.
On another occasion a horse threw an officer.
"Get up, you scoundrel!" Paul shouted. The
officer's leg was broken. Paul spat on him.

Discipline at any cost. The cost was perhaps
excessive. In trussing the troops and exiling
the generals, there was an invitation to defeat.
The thrashings that ensued made Paul morose.
But mobile as madmen are, his humour veered
and he shook a fist at Europe.

"I will fight any sovereign in single combat.
I will fight all of them."

Incidentally, he had become grand-master of the Knights of Malta. The office was useful. When visiting his harem where, with the punctuality of kings, he went every afternoon at four precisely, the office enabled him to wear the Holy Order of St. John of Jerusalem. It was otherwise serviceable. It prompted. With it, he planned to be pope, successor of Pius VI. and the twelve apostles. A decent, unassuming tsar.

A busy one also. The form of a hat, the size of a neckcloth, the colour of a feather, the cut of a coat, one's boots, one's gaiters, a coachman's livery, a horse's harness, became affairs of state, the subjects of ukase. The only printing-press that he permitted to function was one that published his edicts. For a disregard of anyone of them, Siberia!

The droves he sent there, for no reason whatever, except the pleasure of it, perplexed the foreign legates. One of them wrote that, barring the prisons, which were full, Petersburg was becoming a desert, everybody was being exiled. Some were sent to the mines for calling a yacht a schooner. The yacht was a schooner, but it was Paul's and, by imperial ukase, a frigate. Others went for saying that they had the liberty to do this or that. The use of the word liberty was forbidden. It was forbidden to speak of any revolution, even and including that of the earth.

That is an exaggeration. Nothing was forbidden. Tsaral Russia had no synonym for the Hun Verboten. The imperial formula was either Prikazeno—It is ordered, or Ne prikazeno—It is not ordered. Simple formulæ and yet so magical that it was inconceivable that they should not be observed and logically inconceivable. At any infraction, the knout. But an infraction was not a prerequisite. Anything sufficed. Paul thought he would take a walk and said so to a general who remarked that it might rain. What an unpleasant person! The knout!

The knout for him, for everybody, for anything, for nothing at all. After the knout, Siberia, the pilgrimage undertaken in chains. The chains irked. So much the better! The chains made sores. Better yet! For any dog of a Samaritan that attempted to comfort the sufferer, to anoint his sores, to bandage his wounds, the knout!

The writhings under that knout were joys to Paul. "Flog," he ordered. "Flog without mercy." Then gloatingly he would ask:—"Did they howl? Tell me about it." The details supplied, he patted his stomach. "Now send them where they won't find their bones."

A Frenchman was asked what he did during the Terror. "I lived," he replied. During the Pauline terror, Petersburg shammed death as Muscovy had under the khans. When it passed, delight was as insane as Paul. In the frozen streets, beneath the frigid sky, people kissed and romped and danced and sang. An officer ran his horse up on the sidewalk. "Now," he exclaimed, "we can do what we like!" In the first year of the nineteenth century, that was a Russian officer's idea of liberty.

Kant, in defining liberty, said that it consists in obeying those laws only to which we have given our assent. In any autocracy, particularly in the United States, where one has all the forms of liberty and none of the substance, assent is implied. Under the tsars and under the Cæsars, even the forms were lacking. "Your god and master orders it," Domitian, in addressing the servile senate, negligently remarked. Paul's attitude was identical. To heighten it was his dead-cat face. Mediævally, death was a grinning skull topping a nightmare frame of bones, to which philosophy added a scythe and poetry wings. From its eyries it swooped, spectral and sinister. Deduct the rictus and replace the scythe with a knout and that is the manner in which Paul appeared. High and low quaked if he but looked. The sullen streets were empty.

Those who had to be in them, made themselves small, fled at a footstep, dematerialised into shadows. Whatever they did, however they hid, terror stalked them. It stalked all the Russians of all the Russias. It spread as disease spreads, from cities to hamlets, from the provinces to the steppes, from the septentrion to the sea. Ashen-faced, along the roads it ran, calling, "I am Fear!"

Throughout Russia, life, then, was a panic and panic is contagious. Breathe it and even autocrats are infected. It infected Nero. To escape it, he killed himself. It infected Paul. The terror he exuded returning back to its spring, terrorised him. To escape it, he who made others hide, hid from them.

Nero also hid, but he could not hide from himself. Paul fancied that where that monster failed, he could succeed. By day, he did. He got behind ukases, screened himself with them. But at night, the furies were waiting. The creature needed a disguise and he invented one. He discovered, or said he had, how to look seventeen years younger.

One disguise is always inadequate. Another

occurred to him, a domino of granite.   He put
it on, as soon, that is, as it could be made for him.
In the tailoring, an army of masons was employed.   The result, the Michel Palace, was a
threat in stone, a dungeon surrounded by moats,
a fortress so vast that it discouraged adventure
and so sombre that even the furies might lose
their way.   Once a day only and then at high
noon, the drawbridges were lowered.   To the
yodel of horns and the crack of postilions' whips,
the mail was brought.   That service completed,
the drawbridges were raised, the mask was resumed, a threat in stone confronted you.

The threat was effective.   Terror could not
scale it.   Paul was safe.   Yet was he?   From
without, certainly.   But from within?   There
was his wife.   There were his sons.   Who knew
what they might be plotting?   Well, he too could
plot.   At the slightest sign, the axe!   The axe
for all of them.   Meanwhile, a hint.

The hint resumed itself in a *History of Peter
the Great,* which he placed on a table in a room
occupied by his son Alexander.   Paul left the
book open at a page which told of the death of
a tsarevitch, executed for treason, killed at his
father's command.

In spite of the hint, in spite of the threat, in
spite of the disguise, in spite of moats, guards,

sentinels, in spite of all, the furies found him. Paul's nights were terrible. Clearly something else was needed; the iron hand, perhaps. At once, every avenue that led to the palace was barricaded. Martial law was proclaimed. Petersburg became a city abandoned by God, a polar hell, peopled with phantoms but peopled, too, by terror.

Terror, intangible, fluidic, hung in shadows, crept in darkness, lived in silence, sprang from nowhere, vaulted the barriers, leaped at Paul, tore his mask off. Paul, sidling and crouching, screamed. The scream brought Pahlen.

Pahlen, military governor of Petersburg, had a fabulous nose, a cheerful air, nerves of bronze. At the moment he needed them.

"There are conspirators here," the crouching thug spat at him.

How does he know? Pahlen must have wondered.

How he did know is explicable only by the unfathomable acumen which madmen sometimes possess. Yet, there was no secret about it. Everybody, even to the man in the Nevski, knew that a drama was being staged, though not the lines. Those terror wrote and badly as terror always does write. Alexander had adapted them. Pahlen was stage-manager. In the cast were Plato Zubov, ex-Pompadour; Bennigsen, former page of Elisabeth, and a dozen officers, with a regiment for scene-shifters.

With sudden suspicion, Paul pointed. "And you are one of them."

Pahlen saluted. "For your better protection, sir." He fumbled and produced a paper. "Here is the list."

Without looking at the names, Paul straightened. "The axe!"

Pahlen bowed. "They would have had it already, sir, but two of them are your sons."

"Arrest them."

Pahlen wheeled. It was time to act. Beforehand there was supper.

It would have been interesting to have been there. In addition to Paul and his wife, there were a dozen people at table, none of whom was permitted to speak. Elsewhere, in other palaces, there was that rarity, laughter. With it was champagne, lifted glasses, toasts to the actors in the drama staged for that night.

In the supper-room at the Michel Palace there was silence. Presently Paul related a dream he had had and in which he thought he was suffocating. He looked at his wife. Was she on that list? No matter, the scaffold was neighbourly. Comforted by the reflection, he began throwing creams and pastries on the floor. The pages could eat them.

Lampridius, or, more exactly, the brute who abridged him, gave the story of an emperor's death. The lines ring with yells. There is the sudden pretorian rush, the clatter through the Roman palace, the gleam of quick knives.

After supper, Paul went to his apartment, which was on the floor below. Composed of a vestibule, an antechamber, a library and a bedroom, the one entrance was through the vestibule. The bedroom, which was beyond the library, had an exit but that, as additional precaution, had been barricaded. Nearby was a fireplace and before it a screen. At the right was a bed. Above the bed was a picture of a knight of St. John. Opposite was a bust, badly executed, of Frederick II. The room was large, high-ceiled, panelled in white. On the walls were landscapes by Vernet and Van der Meer. In the library there was nothing literary. In the antechamber, two servants, both armed.

On leaving the supper-table, Paul went to bed, to sleep, to dream, to wake, to shriek, to die.

"My God!" said Zubov, "how that man does shriek."

Zubov and the others, all of them, except

Paul's sons, Alexander and Constantine, who were under arrest, had, through interior connivance, crossed the moat, entered the palace, seized and disarmed the guards; after which, rushing up a stairway, they broke into the antechamber and cut down the servants.

Most of them were drunk. The noise they made wakened Paul. When they reached the bedroom they could not find him. They thought he had escaped. But in the rush the screen was overturned. Back of it, up the chimney, Paul's bare feet protruded. They pulled him down. One of them struck him with a gold snuff-box. He shrieked. They ran him through, cutting off three of his fingers while they were at it, he shrieking all the time. In a moment he fell. Another of them, taking him by the head, dashed it against the fireplace, dashed it again and again and then once more.

Afar, a Te Deum mounted. Night refurled her great black fan.

VIII

THE LAST DESPOT

IN Greece, death was a girl. The child of Night, the sister of Sleep, less funereal than narcotic, she beckoned and consoled. In epicurean Rome, death was a marionette that invited you to wreathe yourself with roses before they could fade. In the Muslim east, death was Azrael, who was an angel. In Vedic India it was Yama, who was a god. In Iran it was Mairya, who was a fiend.

That last, and long since forgotten conception, the tsars revived and adopted for others. Elsewhere death had been gracious. In Russia it was horrible.

Alexander altered that. Already Elisabeth had abolished the axe. It was not clemency that actuated her. It was the selfish commonsense which political economy is. Hands without heads cannot work, but heads with hands can and did. They worked for Elisabeth. Instead of a swift decapitation on the scaffold, prisoners were given the slow guillotine of the mines.

The axe which Elisabeth buried there, Nicholas replaced with the gallows. But under Alexander torture ceased.

One may applaud him and very greatly for that, particularly as there is nothing else to his credit. Nothing whatever, except that he was less Asiatic than Paul and more European than Nicholas. Suavity was his note. It is the note of every hypocrite.

Nominally under arrest while Paul was being killed, he pretended to be asleep when the news of it, which he was awaiting, was brought to him. Afterward he pretended that he had nothing to do with it. The pretence served as hot-house for the usual immortelles. Among other garlands is one to the effect that Paul was not his father. However false or true that may be, he did not resemble him. Paul had the sour look of a skunk with a stomach-ache. Alexander looked like a cherub in an overcoat. His brothers, Constantine and Nicholas, did not resemble Paul either, physically, that is, though otherwise they were quite as Tatar, which is not remarkable if their reported geneology be correct. Alexander's father is said to have been an Alsatian grenadier. Their father was a Prussian.

Catherine, who generally knew what she was

ALEXANDER I

about, brought Alexander up to succeed her. Constantine, she brought up to occupy Constantinople. Nicholas, the youngest of the breed, she left to his own devices and very unoriginal they were. At the time of Paul's death he was a brat, the despot in embryo, ruling tin soldiers as he was to rule Russia.

At that time, the earth was oscillating beneath the tread of a human volcano beside whom no nation could live. Hugo, with his usual sobriety, said that Napoleon inconvenienced God. Napoleon would have taken the remark very seriously. Humour, which is Satan's saving grace, he contrived to lack. Napoleon did not inconvenience God, but he disturbed the equilibrium of Europe.

A little before he had run literally from school into a riot, leaped on a horse and made himself general. After which he conquered Italy, conquered Egypt, attacked everybody and vanquished everywhere. A simple tale, it still astounds. In the echoes of his passage come the crash of falling cities, the cries of the conquered, the death-rattle of nations, the surge and roar of seas of blood. Through their reverberations, Napoleon looms, dragging destruction after him, hurling it like a bomb in the face of kings that were cowering still from the spectacle of the

Revolution and of which he was the appalling
issue.

At the time of Paul's death, he was planning
a bout with England. Turning suddenly on
Austria, he sent the old Germanic empire
sprawling. Prussia came next. Then it was
Russia's turn. On a raft in the muddy Nieman,
Alexander pledged him eternal friendship.

Friendship may cover a multitude of rob-
beries. Over the usual question of booty, the
two fell out. Napoleon, meanwhile, had become impersonal. In lieu of the volcanic there
was virulence. He was spreading, as cholera
spreads, from one end of the continent to the
other. In the contagion, was the totter of dynas-
ties, the reversal of thrones. There too was the
victor, pale, impassible as destiny, confronting
fate like an equal, provoking it almost with disdain, peering through magic casements at the
universal monarchy which he dreamed was to
be his.

Into that dream another entered, a minor
dream, the dream of a parvenu. There was
barely a royal residence on the continent which
he had not occupied. There was hardly a sovereign in whose bed he had not slept. For the
vulgar satisfaction of sleeping in one other, he

entered the Kreml. There, beneath a mattress, he left his crown.

In his northern progress, it had been imagined that he would not advance beyond Lithuania, but when he had taken Smolensk, the key to the empire, the eldest town in Russia, Alexander's generals realised that another conversation was inevitable and any resistance vain. Instead of contending, they circumvented. The outlying lands were laid bare. The result is epic. Famine began what ice completed. Napoleon found himself in an empty refrigerator. That refrigerator Alexander burned.

Then began the conversation that continued all along the road to Paris. For climax it had Elba, with Waterloo for finale.

The conversation was not a tête-à-tête. The flames had been a signal. All Europe took part. But in the great débâcle, Alexander greatly rose. He acquired the palms of a hero, the nimbus of a god, a dignity quite Roman, before which the flunkeys of history have solemnly salaamed.

A Greek of the Lower Empire, Napoleon called him, which being translated means a swindler. Good-looking, though, a middle-aged Cupid in whiskers, the burglar tastes of his problematic house fused in him with a sanctimoniousness that was all his own. After the proper tsaral fashion, he had married a German, Betty of Baden. The Comtesse de Choiseul-Gouffier, who wrote of both with a maid-servant's ecstasy, described her as a pathetic angel, tear-stained by the handkerchiefs which, in the exercise of his droit du seigneur, he tossed here and there, yet always so discreetly! Turpitudes in the dark, but never a scandal. Tartuffianism above all.

An oleaginous mummer, Uriah Heep and the Artful Dodger combined, indulgently he agreed to rule in accordance with the law—which he made. With the same benevolence he built schools and universities—on paper, not omitting to stuff his pockets with everything he could lay his hands on, with Finland, of which he robbed Sweden; with the plunder of further burglaries to the south and east; promising a lift to Austria and leaving her in the lurch; doing quite as well by Prussia, who deserved it; hoodwinking everybody, including history, the world and the devil; hoodwinking Napoleon and it was an archcrook who could do that; deceiving perhaps even himself and ending his robber rule in mystic projects and Swedenborgian beliefs.

He might have done worse. Swedenborg lifted fringes of the curtain which recent occultism has partially raised. Alexander's introduction to the *Arcana Celestia* was due to a woman, the Baroness Krudner, whose forte, to put it delicately, had been her weakness. Apoplexy battened on her husband when he learned its extent. The passing of the man brought her the light. The amoureuse became a voyante. She saw. In seeing she foretold the return from Elba, the hundred days, the restoration. Time verified the clairvoyance, which interested Alexander, as well it might, yet particularly perhaps because, in an interview that ensued, the baroness told the emperor—what he already suspected—that he was predestined to accomplish God's will on earth. So are autocrats and mummers won. Alexander took her to Paris, where it is history that she inspired the Holy Alliance, a chimerical imbecility on which, over a century later, the outlines of the League of Nations were ignorantly framed.

Alexander was the silver lining between Paul, who was mad and Nicholas, who was insane. Every silver lining has a cloud. Alexander had brains, a will of his own, the power to use it, the ability to make Russia as preponderant in Europe as Peter had made her preponderant in the north. During the better part of his reign, he drove the empire straight on with the ease of a whip tooling a drag. Personally he had his graces. In spite of a mediæval idea of his own dignity, he could unbend, and, when he did, he charmed. Though a robber, he was a big one. Though a crook, he was great. Even in hypocrisy he contrived to be large. He inspired confidence, and very naturally, he was a confidence man. There is the silver lining.

Here is the cloud. Bossuet defined a heretic as a person who has ideas of his own. Alexander adopted that very advanced view. Already, in connection with the course of the stars, Paul had forbidden the use of the word revolution. Alexander ukased the Copernican system out of the realm. He made it a felony to think. Like Paul, he was mad. The army was sane. In tramping after Napoleon the officers had seen strange things—liberty, which they did not know could be; freedom, which had been unimagined.

These things astounded. Constitutional government amazed. Amazement is the beginning of truth. For the first time, perhaps, officers realised the iniquity of a despotism that made patriotism treason, the folly of having but the right to obey, the nonsense of rescuing Europe from one tyranny while Russia endured another. Such views disorganise.

When they got back, their easy ways and careless talk bewildered. The astounding sans-gêne was incomprehensible. As understanding came, the regeneration which foreign marvels effect was whispered, talked about, talked always a bit louder.

Tsardom had never known a revolution. The hydra waiting for it then was to be killed. Like Dmitri, it had more lives than one.

In the barracks, a plot was hatched. Alexander was to be offered honey on the point of a sword—either a constitution or the fate of Paul. He could take his choice. In sharpening the sword and ladling the honey, the plotters may have been too amateur to appreciate that an autocrat, however autocratic, cannot grant a constitution. An autocrat who is not absolute is a contradiction of terms. Nicholas the Last tried it. He granted a constitution which was so liberal that at any time any Russian could be shot. Among the unconsidered Russians was himself. With him tsardom ceased to be. But though an autocrat must be absolute, he can die. Alexander pretended to. The pomp and pageantry of imperial rites were given to a bogus corpse. Meanwhile, hidden in a monastery at Tomsk, where neither honey-ladlers or history could follow, he cheated amateurs as he had swindled experts.

Night again unfurled her great black fan.

The next in line was Constantine. He refused to move up. He said he lacked the talent. Certainly he did, but he lacked, too, the courage. He was afraid of being assassinated. The fear was not unreasonable. At a review, to show a foreign prince how agreeable it is to be a Russian grand-duke, he drew his sword, marched up to a general and, without a word, ran him through.

Nicholas was next. Like Alexander, he was unlike Paul. But there was nothing cherubic in his appearance. He had the face of the fallen, the scowl of a fiend, a despot's sinister demeanour. History used to regard him as a great man. History saw but the façade. His mind, a rendezvous of zeros, functioned, he believed, altitudinously and only. He had other beliefs, equally inoffensive, yet principally that he was the direct and incarnated emanation of God, the source from which everything proceeded and to which all returned. He believed himself not merely autocrat but omnipotent. Anywhere else, except where he happened to be, he would have been clapped in an asylum.

At this distance, you see the lunatic. On the day he became tsar, he was a hero, to himself that is, yet also to de Custine, a looker-on in

Verona, to whom he related the incidents of the accession, though not all of them, and a few of those which he did relate, he dreamed.

The streets of Petersburg used to be the dreariest and the emptiest in the world. In winter the cold is paralysing. More crippling than cold was dread. The cold came from the pole. It was from the palace that fear's icier fingers stretched.

On that day the Neva was frozen. Flakes of snow were falling, little petals of white roses that were to change to red. But momentarily the sleet of fear had lifted. In addition to roses there was rebellion in the air. Before the palace, suddenly the great square filled. The conspirators that had been eyeing Alexander brought their bayonets there. Beyond, in the converging streets, was that rarity, a crowd. Not one of the crowd, and none of the troopers knew that Constantine had refused to be tsar. In such minds as they had, Nicholas was not next in line, he was out of place. Their leaders had told them that, told them other things also, which, without understanding much of it, they believed.

In front of the palace, on a high pedestal, was a bronze chariot, drawn by winged horses which an enigmatic figure, perhaps that of destiny, led.

On that day its gilded face seemed gay. Perhaps it was. Perhaps, with eyes that saw and foresaw, it was considering, not the pigmy rebels massed below, but a giant that was approaching.

Hoarsely, meanwhile, the prompted pigmies shouted:—"Konstitusia! Konstitusia! Live the Constitution!"

From a window opposite, Nicholas stared. He did not understand. How could he? Coups d'état and palace revolutions there may have been, but soldiers and civilians mutinying in the open streets, that was impossible. It was a moment before his dull brain could grasp it. During that moment, the imperial lupercalia might have ended forever. God save the tsar! About the palace, a sapper regiment was summoned and aligned. Then, from the cavernous porte cochère, out the hero rode. Fancy a shepherd contemplating bleating sheep. That was his attitude. That was the attitude that he dreamed for de Custine's pen.

"On your knees!" he commanded.

In the dream he was obeyed. What followed was not dream, it was in the order of things. Instantly the little white roses changed to red. Mitrailleuses were mowing criminals whose crime was not that they were sheep but that they were parrots. They had been crying for a constitution and at the same time and very sensibly they had been nudging and asking:—"Who is this Konstitusia? Is she Constantine's wife?"

Even otherwise what business was it of theirs? Those that did not die in the streets, died in the Neva, shoved through holes cut in the ice, though some were beaten to death, others peopled Asia and a few were hanged. Among the latter, three fell from the gallows and broke their legs. They were hanged again. Afterward they were decently buried. On their graves, in lieu of the usual cross, Nicholas put little gibbets. "Under Tiberius there was quiet," Tacitus, with dramatic brevity, noted. There was quiet then.

Thereafter the lupercalia became a drama at which you were permitted to assist, but given any disturbance on your part, any remarks, any criticism, any whispering, anything whatever except applause, and out you went, tossed into a sudden grave, or, less fortunately, into a living one. Russia soon discovered that. So did Poland.

Poland still lived, still prayed, murmured occasionally; occasionally, too, fevered with hope, she bandaged her wounds in national rags and sang. The song was of her past. In earlier days, Muscovy had been her vassal. As Russia rose, Poland fell. Three butchers tripped her.

Sharpening their knives, Catherine, the Austrian ruler, the Prussian king, agreed that her body and blood should be a sacrament of communion. Mutilated, dismembered, but not dead, Poland crawled through time to the feet of Nicholas. He stamped on her.

In the atrocities of Caligula there was a reason. He wanted to leave a name that history would preserve. In the atrocities of Nicholas there was also a reason. From history he wanted a name erased. He wanted to exterminate a nation. He deigned to decree—the term is official—that millions should change their language for his, abjure their religion for him. He deigned further to provide a ritual of the worship due to himself. At any objection, the knout, exile, the gallows. Poles were driven in hordes to Tartary, or, more expeditiously, to death. Ten thousand children were taken from their parents, engulfed in Russia, lost there. Rather than have them go, other children were killed by their parents. Like Caligula, Herod also left a name. That of Nicholas exceeds it.

The crime of the revolutionists was that they had tried to think. Poland's crime was that she had succeeded. Nicholas was determined that there should be no thought in Russia save such

as issued from the zeros in his head.   Any other
variety he regarded as atheism.

To prevent the entrance of foes, Ivan ringed
the realm with forts.   To prevent the entrance
of light, Nicholas quarantined it.   Within, Ivan
made a cemetery; Nicholas, a camp.   Immense
improvement.   Petersburg became a parade-
ground of soldiery constantly defiling, a bivouac
in which everything was exacted, nothing permitted and before which, gun in hand, Nicholas
paced like a sentry, guarding the past, challeng-
ing enlightenment, bidding progress begone,
calling at the world:—"Qui vive?"

A German from head to foot, without a drop
of Russian blood, he had married a Prussian,
Charlotte of Hohenzollern, who acquired a mor-
ibund air, the result of being a mother too often.

"S'épuiser en grand-ducs, quelle destinée!"
said de Custine after scrutinising her at a court
ball, which he described as not splendour merely, but poetry.

The high walls were mirrors banked with
flowers, framed with gold, heightened with
lustres, and their effect, which was that of diamond curtains in a shadowless fairyland, turned
the vast hall into a spaciousness where there was
but light and illusion and where the dancers

multiplied themselves indefinitely. It was magical, de Custine added.

Magic is not gaiety. No one laughed, no one talked, people conversed about nothing in whispers. There was constraint there, there was fear, that fear that brooded over Russia and which lurked in the palace of the Cæsars. In the assembly, were kingdomless kings, queens discrowned, slave sovereigns—revivals of the pomps of Rome—and a heat that was Senegambian.

Polar zephyrs annoyed the presiding Teutons. The independence of nature shocked them. De Custine said that the surest way to please Nicholas was to treat Petersburg as though it were Nice and to go about without furs in winter. Flatter the climate and you flattered the tsar, whose intelligence even Victoria regarded as limited.

It would have been pleasant to have seen those two at Windsor. It would have been pleasanter yet to have seen him afterward, when she sent him the ultimatum which was the fanfare to the Crimean war. The ultimatum was delivered to Nesselrode, who was his foreign minister. Nesselrode—to-day a pudding—said that his august lord would not deign to notice it, which was tantamount to telling her to go to hell. It was she who sent him there, more exactly, it was Russia's subsequent allies, England and France.

A very ignorant, a very brutal and—at this distance—a very amusing person, Nicholas none the less was a real figure, not a lay one, an iron man, liberty's exterminating angel, a being who annihilated the goddess whenever she appeared. In that was his glory, such as it is, and, such as it was, for thirty years he sustained it over Russia awed and Europe coerced. For thirty years, Ivan to his people, he was Agamemnon among kings.

Europe, though coerced, could think. It occurred to her that the iron man might be a scarecrow. With Russia it was different. Submissive she lay at the feet of her paradomaniac, who knew but one joy, the sight of troops constantly parading, and but one consolation, the conviction that he was the great I Am. The conviction was an illusion which Europe presently proceeded to ablate. The shock of the loss of it killed him. The story of it all is called the Crimean War.

That inglorious scramble into which England entered with the stern spirit of a policeman and France with the vendetta views of a bandit, began over a question of therapeutics. Nicholas declared that the Sultan was a Sick Man. The diagnosis was his own. By way of regimen, he proposed to break into the patient's room, first finish, then rob him. But though the diagnosis was novel, the second-storey treatment was not.

Constantinople, the old imperial city, Tsargrad as Muscovy called her, had been the secular goal of Slav ambition. Sophia Palælogus, Ivan's grandmother, was a descendant of the final Byzantine emperor. Later tsars regarded themselves as that Cæsar's heir. Russia's historic pretensions to Stamboul had no other origin. In the initial stages of the subsequent world war, it was therefore highly diplomatic of England to think of offering it to her, particularly as she thereby succeeded—and to Germany's glee—in alienating both Bulgaria and Greece. The Coburg adventurer expected to sit there. So also did Constantine and his Hun Klytemnestra.

But, at this time, England could not countenance the Slav ambition. The Dardanelles Russian, the Mediterranean would be a Muscovite lake and Turkey a carpet to the Indus. England could not permit that, nor France either.

France, formerly the most militant of nations, yet then very bourgeois, had her hand forced. The bait of revenge was dangled at her. The dangling was done by Louis Napoleon, who al-

ready had deceived everybody twice—first in
pretending that he was a fool; afterward, in pretending he wasn't. Revenge was not his object.
He wanted to get into society and take his wife
there. More exactly, it was the lady who
wanted him to do both. So much for Helen.
Now for Agamemnon.

Asiatically, with Tatar contempt, the German bastard eyed the Frenchman and asked if
he remembered what Russia had done to the
other fellow. Then the allies went at him.
Sevastopol was their objective. Their object
was less certain. The troops did not know
whether they were for or against the Sick Man,
who was quite as real to them as the Pierrot in
the moon. The high command, better informed
perhaps, was not for that reason overburdened
with intelligence. They thought the serfs
would rise and Sevastopol topple.

Official Russia had an equivalent understanding of the allies. "We have only to shy our hats
at the imbeciles," she carelessly remarked. Half
a century later, her opinion of the Japanese was
as cheerful. "Monkeys with the brains of parrots," they were grand-ducally described. But
though she was not happy in her views of the
coalition, she was happier with it than with

Nippon. The sum total of the allied achievements was the reduction of a single citadel.

That citadel, Sevastopol, the arsenal of the empire, held, behind a veil of forts, a fleet that was to make the Sick Man sicker. Once the arsenal taken and the fleet destroyed, the patient was safe. So argued the allies. Into the Euxine they sailed, on the sacred Chersonese they landed. From heights above the Alma, a river to the north of Sevastopol, the Russians blazed at them. The allies crossed the river, climbed the heights, said, "How are you?" and let them run, which they did, to Sevastopol, bewildered by such civility. To show perhaps that they had not come for mere amenities, the allies went around to Balaklava, on the other side of the arsenal, tried to pound it from there, pounded it, or tried to pound it, from the sea, failing in each effort, finding that instead of a naval excursion, they were confronted by an army then eager to get at them.

That army, at which the Light Brigade made a dash so magnificent that Bosquet exclaimed, "Ce n'est pas la guerre!" and Tennyson, very originally and unobviously added, "Some one had blundered," that army drew the allies at Inkerman into a sublimated Donnybrook Fair, a rough and tumble, in the dark, in the rain, in

which it was beaten but only because the allies
were the bigger gluttons. Of generalship there
was none. English tactics were simple. It was
"Up boys and at 'em." French strategy was
not more complicated, nor was the Russian finer.
But the accounts make very agreeable reading,
so agreeable that, in considering them now, anyone who did not know better might mistake the
Russians for titans and the allies for gods.

Ultimately, the gods muddled through, but
not until they had out-manœuvred the titans'
chief of staff, General February, General Cholera and the usual traitor in the allies camp, General Stupidity. These interfered. So did another strategist, the Weather. Allied ships,
bearing supplies, were overtaken and sunk by
storms marshalled by General February. General Stupidity saw to it that provisions that
eluded the gales either rotted obscurely or else
landed safely in Russian mouths. General
Stupidity, reinforced by General Cholera, arranged that the sick had no succour, the maimed
no aid. Yet, presently, there were correspond-
ents to tell of these things—inkbeasts as Bismarck subsequently called them. Presently,
also, there were angels to relieve—English
women from whose work the Red Cross resulted.

Meanwhile the siege progressed and very curiously. It was a siege that involuted, doubled on itself, presenting an oddity, the spectacle of beleaguers as beset as the beleagued, of forces contending with other foes than each other, of incompetence pitted against corruption. Finally, after routs and heroics, ramparts were scaled, redoubts were taken, Sevastopol fell. It fell as Moscow fell. Like Moscow it was burned. Its sables were shrivelled, its fortresses dumb, the wings of the eagles were clipped.

For the time being that is. Twenty years later Russia was again at the Sick Man. She was at his door. But for the police she would have had him. As it was she got away with a lot of his goods. Said Salisbury admiringly: "We put our money on the wrong horse."

At this time matters were very different. At the crash of the fall of the arsenal, Russia awoke. Humiliated by the presence of hostile legions on her sacred peninsula, dismayed in the Crimea as she was to be in the East, startled by the totter of bastions which official corruption had undermined, aghast at the cries of soldiers to whom that corruption had been the bitterest foe, bereft of her belief in imperial might, Russia rose from her secular slumber and arraigned autocracy at the bar of God.

Nicholas, the iron man, sank back. A cartoonist pictured General February also turning traitor and poking a frigid finger at the emperor's heart. Nicholas had no heart. What he did have was a thoroughly mistaken idea of his own importance. That gone, fright replaced it.

Fright plucked at his sleeve, shoved him to bed, then to his grave, nodded good-riddance, turned to his heirs and destroyed them. Over, beneath, around and about them, it set a tyranny more tyrannic than their own.

Tsars, hitherto, had the freedom that waves possess. Thereafter, behind their own high throne, a higher one stood. In it sat the giant whom the gilded eyes of destiny perhaps foresaw on that day when the white roses changed to red and Nicholas hushed the parrots. The giant was King Terror.

Perhaps Nicholas also foresaw him. He had no imagination, but life is a book that man reads when he dies. In its pages that vanish as you touch them, myopia may become clairvoyance and obtuseness understanding. It may be that from before the flickering eyes of the dying tyrant a veil was lifted. It may be that he saw red hosts trampling tsardom into the things that were, tossing the last of the breed to the bats of a Siberian Avernus. It is said that he did not die of pneumonia, as was officially announced, but of a drug of his choosing. Like books, drugs, too, have their sorceries and his may have shown him that the fate of autocracy is the hell from which it came. But probably it did nothing of the kind. Probably he remained to the end, heavy-witted, unenlightened. Yet if it be true that the dead turn in the grave at what they see, long since he must have been in perpetual motion.

IX

KING TERROR

ROME had other gods than the Cæsars, herds of them, so many that they outnumbered the population. Except a few little gods and one very great divinity, they were all foreigners. Most of them were known to everybody. But not the great god. His name, a secret, only the hierophants knew. A senator was put to death for having uttered it. Engendered perhaps by Pan who engendered Panic, the great god was Pavor—Terror. With him, Rome conquered the world. Then he turned and tore her.

The history of Russia is an expurgated edition of that of Rome. There are blanks in it. One blank is nine hundred years long. The rest is the chronicle of an orgy at which autocrats feasted longly. After Sevastopol, history turned, reversing the orgy, putting the table on top and despots beneath, revealing to their cowering eyes one greater than they, the old god who then was king. He, too, could feast and from their cups of mud and blood he tore them.

The first Nicholas escaped him only by dying. Yet such was the shock of the sight of his face, that that hangman, who was Liberty's executioner, gibbered, "Emancipation!"

Here enters his son, Alexander II. History shows how the great monarch dogged him; how he shadowed his successor; how he annihilated the last of the lot; how disinterring the forgotten, he instituted a despotism more destructive than theirs and became an evocation of Genghiz. Attila wanted to destroy civilisation. Genghiz wanted to destroy humanity. Terror can be quite as gentle.

There is an odd tale of a wizard who kept in a bottle an imp that he worshipped. One day the imp got out and slew him. Terror resembles that imp. Terror used to be a fetish of the tsars. The day came when the fetish was headsman. In history as it is written, the second Alexander was killed by a bomb. That is a superficial view. An autocrat was killed by his ikon.

A tall German, with a heavy jowl, a receding forehead, a cavalry moustache and mutton-chop whiskers, Alexander II. was the portrait, in blood, of Nietzsche's blonde beast. Like Nietz-

sche, he had frequented the antique sages.
When anything annoying confronted them, they
confronted it, waved it away, denied its existence. Excellent tactics. Alexander employed
them on Poland. Drugged with the poppies of
her eternal hopes, Poland rose up before him.
With a stare, he blighted her.

After Poland, nihilism. In between—and
the margin has the width of years—stood the
Porte. The tsar stared at the sultan who stared
back. Abdul the Damned was quite as vulper-
ine as any other autocrat and considerably more
astute. "Time and I against all comers," was
the motto that hung in the Yildiz Kiosk. He
was ill though, sick with the same malady that
Dr. Nicholas had diagnosed. Yet, invalid
though he were, he liked to bundle Christians
off the earth. It distracted him. Gladstone
could not stand that nor, to Gladstone's disgust,
could Alexander.

Alexander cared nothing about Abdul's
amusements. Former tsars had dispatched too
many Christians for additional dispatches to vex
him. But the tsaral heritage, the antique Greek
throne, the immemorial desire to slake an imperial thirst in the waters of the Golden Horn,
that was another aria, highly melodious, yet held
profane in the European Sunday-school con-

cert. The familiar and altruistic hymn concerning the purification of St. Sophia was much more decorous and entoning it he marched Skobeleff against Abdul, who countermarched, nearly marched over him and then marched back, farther, farther still, from the Shipka Pass and Plevna to San Stephano and the slim gilt gates of Stamboul.

Skobeleff had him. Byzantium, the imperial houri, Roman in body but Greek in soul, whose fair beauty even the ferocious apostolicism of the Turks could not wholly mar, was in his grasp. At that moment British ironclads entered the Dardanelles. •Skobeleff snapped his fingers. Alexander commanded him to glove them and salute. Skobeleff's anger was Homeric. It shook the legions. They adored him. With them he would have taken Alexander and hanged him. The Cæsars had their brews. So had the tsars. Skobeleff, hero of Plevna, a national idol, was poisoned. History can only record it. History is an endless book. Nihilism was writing a page in it then.

Nihilism, mother of bolshevism, came, as her daughter came, from Germany. A simple creed, it held that the happiness of mankind requires the abolition of everything. Assuming that to be true, happiness remains to be defined, which it never has been, except by Voltaire, who called it a myth invented by Satan for man's despair. Utopia is perhaps as mythical and general happiness a chimera. General contentment seems less illusory. Its main factor, perhaps, is non-interference and that may come when man shall have learned that nothing is important.

Nihilism is a term that a saint invented. In the *De civitate Dei*, Augustin said:—*"Nihilisti appelantur quia nihil credunt et nihil docent."* Nihilists believe in nothing and teach it.

Russian nihilism first took shape after the Crimea. After San Stephano, it took substance. Weening, trundling, training it, was old King Terror.

Nihilism, originally a theory, afterward a doctrine, became a force. The theory interested, the doctrine impressed. The force developed a generation new to Russia, a generation that thought. To think was always forbidden and very unnecessarily. No one dreamed of such a thing. Besides, it was a depraved occupation. It induced disease. It induced it then. It caused a form of neurosis of which poverty of the blood and empty pockets were contributory. The new generation lacked food. In the open, before the palace, it cried for reform. Alexander stared. The cries redoubled.

Alexander deigned to admonish. Solemnly, he stated that reforms come not from below but from above.

He might have added that revolutions display the same phenomena. He might have explained that the Convention was the work not of plebeians but of philosophers. He might have shown that in France, after everything had been demolished, everything was rebuilt. He might have demonstrated that in the upheaval only names were changed, that instead of a king by right divine, there was a dictator by might infernal.

These platitudes he could have adorned with anecdote. But, son of an iron man and father of another in an iron mask, he was not otherwise ironic. He lacked the wit to deduce the paradox that Russia could be worse off than she was and the humour to declare that he would facilitate it. In circumstances such as confronted him, it was the fashion of his house to turn everybody into mincemeat. Instead of decimating, he vacillated; instead of jesting, he promised. To his subsequent regret that promise he kept. Freedom was tossed to the people like a bone to a dog. Forty million human chattels had an in perpetuum mortgage on them lifted.

Former tsars gave them away by the thousand and as readily as a snuff-box. They were won and lost at cards, auctioned with furniture and cows, sold with lands designated as "inhabited estates." Actually chattels, descriptively serfs, technically they were souls—when male. A woman had no soul. With Alexander's permission she acquired one. It was very considerate of him. But to the owners, robbed of their goods, the whole thing was a despotic caprice. To the manumitted it was confusing. The bone they got was bare as your hand. Was it even a bone? They had their doubts. To their lords they had been accustomed to say:—"We are yours, but the land is ours!"

Abruptly, through some legerdemain, they ceased to be anybody's, the land ceased to be theirs, apparently free to come and go, they had nowhere to go to. The earth had opened. All that remained was their hovels, where they could continue to starve—on paying for the privilege. If that was liberty, they preferred slavery. More exactly, they preferred to believe that somewhere, very far no doubt, but somewhere, the little father on a high throne sat waiting and willing to give them such land as they needed. Otherwise, what did this word emancipation mean?

Nihilism explained. Emancipation meant that for land to be free it must first be manured with the blood of mythical Romanovs. There are explanations that do not explain. There are also natures that are not receptive. To the people, the Romanovs, however mythical, were sacrosanct, quasi if not wholly divine. The idea is absurd, but the absurder an idea the more fanatics it can claim. The certainties of mathematics are not exciting, but for chimeras nations have fought and died. What is more remarkable, they have drudged. Russia had drudged too long for the tsars to turn on Alexander. Even otherwise the manumitted were dull. Ages of despotism had not soured their minds. They had none. They had only a few wants reduced to a minimum, a few instincts knavish and primitive. They liked to get drunk. They liked to rob. But for the knout they had a pathetic respect; they had an inherited hatred of novelty, and an ingrained awe of the tsar. To such as they, the explanations of nihilism were as wind on the steppes. Ideas could not be planted on wastes that so long had been bare. What tyranny had not stirred, theory could not affect.

Nihilism, outfaced by stolidity, wheeled.

From the peasant, it turned to the palace. Islam had converted with the sword, the Inquisition with the stake, the Convention with the guillotine. Demonstrations being futile, nihilism took to dynamite. Murder clubs mushroomed in Petersburg. Autocracy became a despotism tempered by bombs.

Between the foregoing sentences there are years. There are concessions, too—of the kind that put Louis XVI. in the tumbril. Like that imbecile, Alexander II. had inherited a situation which he had not created. He differed from him in every other respect. America called him Lincolnoffski. Europe was salaaming to him for his treatment of the Turk. He had a government of iron, a people absolutely subservient. In between was but a thin red line.

To efface that line Alexander did his best, and also his worst. He used all means to conciliate; those failing, all means to suppress. Nihilism already outfaced by stupidty, indifference might have squelched. Indifference is highly coercive. But though Alexander had frequented the antique sages, he had also loitered over the annals of his house. When philosophy deserted him, ferocity stepped in. Moreover, the courage which previously he had lacked, Plevna supplied. Young men who had just left the universities were given post-graduate courses in Siberia. Young women, less advanced perhaps, were taught that of all brutes, pliocene, miocene, lampsacene, the most ignoble is man. These lessons, instead of correcting, corroded. After each deportation to Siberia, when it did not happen to be Shame, the places of the exiles were filled, and so fully that you would have thought that terrorists covered the land. Generated spontaneously, multiplying with the rapidity of insects, swarming everywhere, they presented a curious spectacle, the infinitely little contending with the infinitely great.

To Petersburg, then, came larger prisons. To the mines were longer lanes. In the mines was the dry guillotine; in the prisons there was torture, the rack re-established, applied for nothing, for a look, for a word, for holding a pamphlet, for throwing it way. Very properly, too, and with the finest sense of law and order. Defendants were tried in public. What more could they ask? It is true they were always convicted. But what did they mean by looking, by talking, by having or not having things in their hands? To teach them better, torture followed. The torture was private. To make it more private the condemned were never seen again. If they had been, perhaps only their mothers could have recognised them.

Then, face to face, were two terrors; the white terror radiated by the tsar; the black terror radiated at him.

One does not choose between tears, or perhaps between terrors. Yet of those two terrors, the more terrifying was the black. The white terror terrified the little. The great, being large, are more receptive. The mighty were terrified most.

Black terror is nihilism in its acute form. Usually maniacal, sometimes in its delirium it has expressed that which was inarticulate in a nation. Always hideous, sometimes it is sublime. In France, it had been grandiose. But Russia lacked a Mirabeau; the terrorists, a Danton; the people, a Voltaire, who, even if they had had him, they could not have read. They were otherwise blessed. With them, to a man, was the imperial clan.

The latter, violently opposed to Alexander's concessions, saw in reform a diminution of themselves. Peter would have devoured the lot. Alexander lacked the stomach. By policy a philanthropist, though by instinct a thug, physically scrofulous and mentally unsound, congenitally aphasiac and consequently incoherent, freeing Russia and regretting the act, history, with her gallery taste for shams, saw what she could mistake for the righteous liberator and applauds him still. No one need begrudge him that. For the first time since tsars were invented, the orgy palled. In what otherwise would have been his normal enjoyments, terrorism interfered, absolutism as well.

Whether the two combined in uncertain. In the tenebrous chronicles of the great carnivora there is always much that is obscure. But in his court, which of all courts was the most regal, he became afraid to stir. One evening, it was fortunate for him that he omitted to.

Long before he had married a Hessian. On that evening she was ill. Another lady presided. This other, the Favorita, was the Princess Dolgorouki, whom presently, when the Hessian was dead, he married and who, at the time, had a court of her own.

Without, in the hollow square that fronted the palace, cavalry was stationed. Within, on a wide stair, ran a hedge of rose-tunicked Cossacks, a line of Circassians in silver and pale blue. Beyond that rainbow, in a red-gold hall, which a thousand candles lit, was this man, his mistress and their court. Where the cavalry were was ice, a wind that had knives. Within,

in the glowing hall, was the atmosphere of a
seraglio perfumed with turpentine and Russia
leather—an odour which this palace always exhaled. From above, in a gallery, fell a tinkle
of balalaikas, accompanying the conversation
which must have been dull. Adjacently, or
more exactly, less than a quarter of a mile away,
was another hall, equally pleasant, where these
people were to dine.

Like the conversation, the minutes dragged.
The tsar, the princess, the court, were waiting
for a German, a boor, one of the Hesse tribe,
who was guest that night. Finally, a breath, a
rumour, an announcement. The royal brute
strode in. The usual brilliancies. The forma-
tion of the usual procession, which, just as it
started, shook.

Lights flared, the hall oscillated, mirrors fell.
Into the scented atmosphere came another
odour, a trifle acrid, the smell of smoke which a
concussion had preceded. From a guard-room,
directly beneath the dining-hall, terrorists had
blown up the table, blown off the ceiling, killed
the guard below, the pages above, sixty in all.
An unpunctual Hun had saved the tsar that
night.

The night was in February, 1880. A year
passed during which other attempts were made,

but not without the police knowing beforehand that they would be. In the subsequent reign, the third Alexander saw an officer of his household approaching and, not recognising him, shot him dead. The second Alexander also saw a man approaching and also fired. It was at himself that he shot, at his figure reflected from a mirror. Enviable existence.

Presently it was learned that he was to inspect the troops. As he might go one way and return another, or vice versa, at both ways two men, each with a bomb, were stationed. Afterward it was said that the explosive employed looked and smelt like honey. If that be true, a new and fragrant death was hurled at him in two bombs, both of which, wrapped in cotton, looked like snowballs. The second bomb killed the terrorist and the tsar. What remained of Alexander II. was removed on a carpet.

In a very human effort to avoid that bomb, Alexander, a few days before, had arranged to placate terrorism with a constitution. To placate is to disarm—but not everybody. That which may pacify one, can infuriate another. It may be that, in planning a sop to Cerberus, he aroused another dog. Yet, in any event, previously, there had been minor precautions.

To prevent the entrance of foes, Ivan ringed

the realm with forts. To prevent the entrance
of ideas, Nicholas established a quarantine. To
prevent the entrance of death, Alexander put
police. Incoming ships were searched, incoming travellers stripped. Bales of tea, brought
on camels from China, were turned inside out.
For an incautious word, the mines! On the
vaguest suspicion, the gallows!

To death, what were these precautions? It
had not quite got him yet, but terror had and so
potently that this man who was potent also,
signed a ukase convoking a national assembly.

It is said that Alexander's son protested. He
was put under arrest. It is said that Alexander's brother also protested but, more adroitly,
to others than the tsar. It may be a coincidence
but promptly the honeyed death was served.
Similarly, it may be another coincidence that
the ukase, already in type, disappeared. But
it is a fact that absolutism remained.

After one Alexander, another. After a scrofulous father, a scrofulous son, a composite being
at once Torquemada and Jack the Slipstring, a
sceptred prisoner projecting death from his cell
and feeding on fear, a hulking giant strong
enough to fell an ox and afraid of his shadow,
an obese butcher with the brains of a mujik and
the virulence of a plague.

A younger son, he had not been awaited or desired on the throne. The death of a brother, then his father's, put him there. He did not want it. Reigning over Russia, once the grandest of mundane vocations, terrorism had divested of any charm. The savour of the orgy had gone. As grand-duke, if he knew little else he knew at least that. But into dull brains dreams will creep. He fancied that he had been miraculously chosen to incarnate the theocratic power which his father said, and not only said but believed, was a gift personally bestowed on him by the Almighty. He fancied that the sacrament of coronation induced regeneration and that in the attending hypostasis he would be transformed into a god.

It is unbelievable, but everything is unbelievable in this creature who managed to be both a nigger king and a state prisoner and who, however he may be regarded, supped terror with a long spoon. That terror he felt it his divine mission to disperse. Dissent was, he imagined, the cause, and dissent meant to him everything that was not orthodox and illiterate. Terrorists, nihilists, Jews and Gentiles, he jumbled confusedly in what little mind he had. They were all abominable in the sight of Heaven, vermin that it was for him, as Heaven's emanation, to destroy. Piously and austerely he began, for pious and austere he was.

Pobiedenostsev, procurator of the holy synod, a thin-lipped hyena with a vulture's beak, catered diabolically to that piety. In submitting measures, diabolic in themselves, he always cited a text from the Bible. Vichnegradski, minister of finance, a clever rogue, heard of it and cited two texts. He impressed the tsar greatly. Dagmar of Denmark, Alexander's wife, a gentle soul, gentle at least by comparison with him, cited texts also and cited them but once. Charity is the New Testament told in a word. In connection with his Judenhetze she reminded him of it.

"Ah, yes, my dear," the sanctimonious Nebuchadnezzar replied. "But we must never forget that it was the Jews who crucified our Lord."

The Jews did nothing of the kind, but that is another page from the arcana celestia, in addition to being beside the issue, which this man made very poignant. His father had established courts where defendants were at least tried in public. The son abolished them. Then the Jew baiting began.

At the time there were five million Jews in Russia, exactly five million too many, almost every one of whom was more intelligent than the emperor. They were evicted, despoiled, plundered, hounded and hunted into pariah communities, piled in on top of one another like grasshoppers in a ditch. Here and there were priests' hunts. The Judenhetze was everywhere. It would have been joy to him could he have destroyed them all. Nor was Israel alone afflicted. The attitude of the fourteenth Louis to the Huguenots was courteous by comparison to the third Alexander's treatment of the Lutherans. In Nero, Christianity had a foe less malign than he. He issued edicts that would have penalised the Apostles, ukases that would have outlawed the Christ. At any criticism in the *Times,* which Dagmar read, he foamed at the mouth. Had the editors been in Russia their shrift would have been short.

"They are a set of hogs," he wittily remarked.

Yet it was this man that kept Europe at peace. The dishwashers of history have said that his motive was religious. The motive, less spiritual than physical, was due to the fact that a fat tyrant, afraid of nothing but danger, did not care to incur the risk and discomfort of mounting a horse. He had other risks to consider. Barring his father, no modern monarch had more. Barring his son, no autocrat led a life such as he.

ALEXANDER III

In Petersburg, when he drove, a cloud of
Cossacks enveloped him. The empty streets
were swept. No one was permitted there.
When he journeyed, it was over rails uninter-
ruptedly guarded, minutely patroled. The route
was a lane of troops. The train, divided into
four sections, made it difficult to conjecture in
which of them he hid. But not impossible.
The right one was dynamited. From the wreck
he disentangled his wife, his daughter and himself. About them were guards dead and dying.
The girl, flinging herself at him, cried:—"Oh,
papa, now they will come and murder us all!"

At that cry, the charwomen of history have
wept. But at the cries of countless children
whom this Nebuchadnezzar devoured, not a
word. Perhaps it was a negligible detail. But
though terrorists did not again alarm the girl,
they had not done with him. Terror, more con-
stant than they, had not either.

Thereafter, his residence became a secret. On
his palaces flags flaunted, but, among them all,
where he was, Russia did not know. In town,
his home was a fortress; in the country, a bas-
tille. Approach to either was impossible.
Every avenue was guarded. Every hour the
guard was changed. Princes, who happened to
be stopping at one or the other of them, were

forbidden at any time, night or day, to lock their door. However becoroneted their belongings, they were searched.

Visits were not encouraged. The man fought shy even of his relatives. He knew them. On an Easter egg he found a terrorist threat; in a family album a terrorist face. In spite of patient precautions, death's-heads fluttered in the dreary halls through which he slunk, a hangman shaking at shadows, an emperor who continued to be executioner but who had ceased to be tsar, a monarch turned mole, burying himself behind walls which could not shelter him from fright, invoking saints and signing the death-warrants of officers of his household, leaving to take care of itself an empire which he was no more fitted to rule than a sea-serpent is competent to be an apothecary, going mad before going to his Maker, driven mad by one who had come unawares as thieves and angels do.

The visit, a little drama in itself will be told in a moment.

Meanwhile, Israel agonised. In a district where other game was scant, a prince hunted Jews. One appeal remained, it was to God. In secret synagogues, the candles were reversed and in the name that contains forty-two letters; in the name of the Tetragrammaton; in the name of the Globes and the Wheels; in the name of Him who said, "I am that I am and who shall be," the great ban, Schammatha, was pronounced. Ofanim were implored to repeat the malediction. Jehovah was supplicated to rain on the tsar every curse in the Roll of the Law. The Lord of Hosts was adjured to blot him out from under the sky.

In the Orient, mantras are believed to be effective. Russia was always Asiatic. The incantations of the secret synagogues vibrated, ascended and perhaps were heard.

At Livadia, the emperor fell ill. The ailment was slight, an attack of coryza, which normally lasts a week, unless the patient is carefully tended, in which event it may persist. The imperial coryza persisted and pleurisy developed.

In Moscow, at the time, was a specialist, eccentric and successful. His name was Zakkarin. Summoned to the Crimea, he came and diagnosed. It would have been interesting to have seen him at it. If he had been a terrorist he could have killed the tsar and been torn to bits the next minute. Zakkarin was not a terrorist. He was a physician. As physician he prescribed a remedy which, precautionally, he had brought. Uncomplainingly, the august patient deigned to take it. Zakkarin was looking at him.

It would have been still more interesting to have seen that look. Shakespearian, disquieting and yet serene, it was a look that said, "At last!"

There was not much room in the camp-cot which the third Alexander habitually used, but in it, from before that look, he shrank.

Beside him, stood the physician. The room, vast, high-ceiled, furnished in the large Victorian manner, was covered with wall-paper manufactured in Manchester to frighten children. Behind Zakkarin, was Dagmar. Behind her was the procurator of the holy synod, together with an officer of the household. In the hall were servants. Beyond were guards. Without, enveloping the palace, was a sotnia of Cossacks. Yet, unperceived, unheralded, unannounced, with no show of royal honours, a great king had come.

The emperor, unaware as yet of that, but subconsciously stirred, poked his head at the physician.

"What are you?"

Zakkarin, leaning forward, whispered it. "A Jew."

"A Jew!" the obese butcher shrieked.

Zakkarin turned and explained. "His majesty is delirious."

He turned anew to his patient and whispered again. "You are doomed."

Alexander, to shriek his fright, had raised himself. But the whispers were potent. More potent still was the drug. He fell back. The ban, too, had fallen. Israel had triumphed where terrorism failed.

"Weep, Russia!" ran the official notice in the next issue of the *Novoye Vremya*. "The emperor is dead!"

Zakkarin was given the Nevski decoration and the usual diamonds. In derision, he accepted them.

Another Te Deum mounted. But the orgy, long since embittered, was drawing to a close.

X

THE WHIRLWIND

IT has been said that England conquered half the world in a fit of absent-mindedness. A fit of abstraction, let us say. While England abstracted, Russia absorbed. She absorbed steadily, stealthily, civilly, avoiding noise and offence. Her policy, the most unscrupulous and successful in history, was one which there was no change of administration to alter, no incoming government to reverse. Technically what the tsar willed, it consisted in considering the end, never the means, in turning treaties into memoranda of agreements that were not to be kept, in retreating the better to advance, in avoiding haste but ever forward, in transforming an obscure principality into an empire that covered one-seventh of the land surface of the globe.

Relatively untrammelled and very gay, until latterly it was a round of festivities, soirées in the fairyland of Scheherazade that were followed by a frog dance through Manchuria.

Not so long ago either. One can still hear the admirable orchestra of a nation, apparently invincible, executing Slav airs in Cathay, serenading the dowager, singing to her that they were natural affinities, that, under the khans, Muscovy and Mongolia were one. En sourdine, were roulades not intended for her ear, blythe airs that told of a state dinner in the Forbidden City, with after revels in Delhi and Stamboul.

Quelle rêve! Too fair though, at any rate for Russia, thought the Wilhelmstrasse, where also hung that opium dream.

Obliquely, China eyed them both. The dowager of nations, the eldest of realms, anterior to every monarchy and indifferent to all, she has sat in history aloof, her robes of silk about her, in an attitude of supreme disdain. Beside her arts and wiles, those of dead Greece and buried Rome were modern creations. Before Nineveh, before Eridu and Ur, China was. She has had all time, as these have had their day. The rise of kingdoms, the fall of empires, left her unmoved. Russian cajolements and Prussian snares might disgust, her repose remained unaltered.

At the time, the Shah of Persia, the Shah-an-Shah, King of kings, Regent of the Prophet, was a spider in Russian jelly. The winged bulls that guarded the palaces of Xerxes and of Darius were dead. Turn as he might from them to Mekka, he was doomed. Doomed, too, was that other venomous insect, the Shadow of God on Earth, who throned in Stamboul.

Already, in Afghan passes, Cossacks were peering at the gates of Herat. At a signal, they would have occupied Kabul and fought on and down perhaps, or tried to fight, to the monkey-haunted temples of Benares and the blue gulf of Bengal. It is improbable that they could have got there. Yet, given that signal and the history of the world might have changed. The powers invisible willed otherwise. What they willed, Napoleon perhaps foresaw.

"Prussia," said Napoleon, "will develop into a Germany reconstituted, but that phase will be brief. Anarchy will throw her back where she began. Austria will crumble, Italy become united, and the rôle of France be intellectual."

Napoleon added:—"The supremacy of the world will be divided between England, mistress of Africa, and Russia, established at the Golden Horn."

In Russia, everything goes wrong. That is her history. Her history is an uncompleted book. In some future chapter Napoleon's prediction may come true. "Watch Russia," an adept admonished when the war of the world began. "Great things are gestating there."

Meanwhile, in the gaieties of the Muscovite revel, Germany urged Japan to interpose. Japan needed no urging. A dozen years or so before, she sprang at China, threw the old lady down, and would have pulled her clothes off, had not the police interfered. What Japan had then in view she subsequently acquired, with Wilson's blessing. But at the time, Russia got in the way, not omitting while she was at it, to subtilise a few odds and ends from the dowager's handbag.

To Japan that was highly unjust. The view is amusing. Russia and Japan were like two dogs over the same bone, only, of the two, Russia had the bigger teeth. The teeth were false, but so perfectly adjusted that perhaps Russia herself did not suspect it, though certainly Japan did.

Japan, affecting her usual naïveté, backed away, yet inwardly ravening, nursing her suspicions, her grudge, her arsenals, her warships, her Togo, until—Banzai!—the guns popping at Port Arthur disclosed to a bewildered world the gigantic humbug of Russian might.

Nikolai the Last was then at Tsarskoie Selo, occupied with the puerilities of his empty mind.

The war did not matter. Word was brought him that his fleet was destroyed. At the moment he was playing tennis. Without interrupting the game, he remarked that it was a fine day.

The attitude, curious in itself, was characteristic. In any crisis, he displayed it. When told that he must abdicate, his composure was identical. When arrested he was equally unmoved. A prisoner in his own gardens, his equanimity endured.

Such an attitude is beautiful. But in his case it proceeded not at all from the impassibility of the sage, nor yet from the serenity of the philosopher, but from the indifference of the witless, unless it were the apathy of the drugged.

In an interview that appeared—shortly after the fall of the empire—in the *Novoye Vremya,* Prince Youssoupov, a young man related to the imperial clan, said that Nikolai Alexandrovitch was usually under the influence of a drug which a Thibetan lama had supplied and which was administered by his wife.

None the less he could be witty. Relatives of his wrote, begging him to be merciful to a kinsman. Admirably he replied that their audacity in addressing him was amazing. Admirable, too, was his retort to petitioners humbly

praying for a less rigorous régime:—"Don't in-
dulge in senseless fancies."

These epigrams and that attitude serve in a
measure to delineate the messiah of the Hague
Convention, which Dr. Dillon called an ignoble
farce, and which was designed to jockey Europe
into peacefully disarming while peacefully Russia armed.

Shifty and shallow, physically and mentally
incapacitated even for military duty, his incompetence was so adequately estimated that, before
the great ban was pronounced on his father, he
was sent on a junket through the Orient, where,
in some tiger-hunt, perhaps, he might decently
succumb. In Japan he nearly did. An assault
was made on him there, though whether it were
prearranged or not, one may surmise and never
know. Then indolently the gorgeous East dis-
gorged the offered prey. Clearly he was destined to renew the orgy, to drink and make
merry, though not to his fill. In view of the
fashion in which the cup was torn from him,
there is little in history more curious than an
incident that occurred at his coronation and
which exactly paralleled an incident that happened at the coronation of Louis XVI. On each
occasion the blood of thousands cascaded.

Otherwise it were interesting to have been at

Moscow when the tsar appeared. In a dark uniform, on a pale horse and pale himself from the fast that preceded any coronation, the last and least of the great carnivora rode in. Behind him, in a gilded coach which an imperial crown surmounted, his mother came, bowing to the right, to the left, with a grace mechanical but sovereign. Already she had recovered from the loss of her Nebuchadnezzar. Behind her, in another gilt coach, but minus the crown which as yet was withheld, the tsaritsa sat, rigid, disdainful, her mouth contracted by lines that were to change her face, then singularly beautiful, into a tragic and wasted mask. Along the route, rigid also, but very gorgeous, glittered the imperial guard. Back of these swarmed the stage-managed unwashed. Above was the turquoise of the mid-May sky.

In the Kreml, on the morrow, the archaic, fastidious and highly poetic ceremonial was ministered to a weak young man, for whom the crown was too heavy—in the same manner that, at Rheims, the sixteenth Louis found his crown too big—and who, bent beneath its weight and that of the bullion on his cloak, dropped the sceptre, which any gypsy could have foretold he was destined to drop again. Beside him his bride, born Alix of Hesse, but then Alexandra

Feodorovna of All the Russias, stood erect, her triply tiara'd head unbowed.

Afterward, in the glowing and legendary pomp of long ago, the couple emerged on a terrace, draped with imperial purple and cloth of gold, where they looked on the trained and kneeling crowd beneath, and where an eye-witness, Marie of Rumania, likened them, in their youth and splendour, to the young divinities of old Greece.

The comparison, trite perhaps, is not inapt. On that day, at that moment, both leaned from a parapet of the ideal. The parapet was very fragile. On that day, throngs of the lowly that had come to acclaim, remained to die. Herded together, they were trampled to death. The reign which that day began in blood, ended as bloodily. In it were whole scenes re-enacted from the history of Louis XVI.

Only the interludes differ. Yet, even there, there are similarities. From the old memoirs of the old French court, magicians peer. Through them passes the enigmatic figure of Cagliostro whom, in the court of Nicholas II., Rasputin aped.

In the Winter Palace and afterward when, for a reason that will be recited, that palace was abandoned, crystal-gazers, astrologers, soothsayers were ceaselessly employed, until, Rasputin supervening, they were thanked and dismissed.

In the interim, minor events occurred. The tsaritsa who had snubbed everybody, including Victoria R. I., contrived to present the curious spectacle of an empress boycotted in her court. Perhaps there is no debt more faithfully acquitted than that of contempt, and the disdain which this woman dispensed was such that, barring officials and other people too servile to be affronted, those commanded to court-functions neglected to appear. Had these negligences been confined to a few, the manners of the negligent might have been corrected in the finishing school that Siberia was. But the penalising of all the aristocracy being, not impossible certainly, but perhaps injudicious, the Winter Palace which, the Vatican alone excepted, was the largest and most regal residence extant, became a haunt of caretakers, a haunt, too, of ghosts.

The domestic life of the sovereigns was, meanwhile, eminently correct. Nikolai Alexandrovitch, a model husband, maintained and very sumptuously a lady of the ballet. Therewith, a devoted father, he had but one regret. He lacked an heir. To comfort him, the birth of the tsarevitch was mediumistically foretold,

though, it may be that in the child's advent,
Prince Orlov collaborated. So at least it has
been said. It has been also said that the boy's
potential ability to have children of his own an
anarchist eliminated.

These tales may be untrue. What exceeds
them is the spectacle of an empress owned by
a peasant. Rasputin dominated, that woman
who, domineering herself, dominated her husband. Yet that could not have been difficult.
Without any will of his own, without any ideas
except such as concerned his prerogatives and,
like the Emperor Claudius—Messalina's husband—always of the opinion of the one who
spoke last, which, in this instance, was the tsaritsa, Nikolai Alexandrovitch presented a perfectly defined case of aboulia. It was not he
who ruled, it was his wife, whom Rasputin governed. At a gesture from the latter, policies
were altered, measures reversed. At a gesture,
anyone, no matter what the rank and the higher
the better, was dismissed. At any remonstrance,
exile.

In the gardens of Tsarskoie Selo, there was a
chapel and, under it, a crypt beautified with
Byzantine art, with jewelled marvels, with bro-
cades which the centuries had faded; a crypt
mystically embellished and of which the peace

was stirred only by the choir in the chapel above. There, the haughtiest woman on earth consorted with an ignoble and sinister satyr.

Rasputin entered history, dramatically, in a murder and, quite as dramatically, vacated it, murdered in turn. Originally a vermin-eaten peasant and always a venomous brute, the murder with which he was associated singularly resembled the one related by Erckmann-Chatrian in the *Polish Jew*. The details are nearly identical, except that while, in the novel, the criminal went mad, Rasputin went free—to become a prophet, a saint, possessed, as he pleasantly described himself, by the Holy Ghost.

In spite of which, in spite too of practises that only reticences can convey, he rose, as Peter's laundress rose, on the escalator of fate, from the soil to the throne. There he was waited on by the dignitaries of the empire, as Zubov was valeted by the princes of the realm. In him the Pompadour lineage revived. For the first time in history, a mujik was tsar.

A swarthy blackguard, thaumaturge and comedian, his power over the empress was due to two factors, perhaps to three. The third may have been the woman's dementia. Apart from that, Rasputin possessed the coercive spells of magnetism and clairvoyance. The other fac-

ALIX OF HESSE
WIFE OF NICHOLAS THE LAST

tor, and probably the most potent, was a doctrine that he advanced as his own but which, a century earlier, Boileau summarised as the enjoyment in paradise of the pleasures of hell.

The doctrine, known as quietism, originated with Molinos, a Madrilene monk. Morbid as was everything that came from Spain, it held that temptations are the means employed by God to purge the soul of passion; that to mortify the flesh it should be gratified; that in the omnisapience of the divine, man is saved not merely by righteousness but by evil, by crapulence as well as continence.

These tenets which Rasputin imposed, were accepted by the empress in that crypt, where she was followed by her daughters, whose governess, Mademoiselle Toutschev, complained to their father that Rasputin visited them at night. Whether actual relations occurred is obscure and unimportant. It has been more or less authoritatively stated that they did occur and whether the statement be true or false, it was one of the causes that led to the mujik's death.

At the time, as in Rome before the fall, everything was for sale. Before the fall of the Russian empire, place, power, army contracts, ministerial portfolios, everything, the virtue of women, the honour of men, the defense of the realm, everything was up for auction, except the throne and that only because in it sat the auctioneer, who had to sit somewhere pending its projected sale to curio-collectors in the Wilhelmstrasse.

Before that could occur, in the streets, theatres and basilicas of the capital, the national anthem was sung. The anthem was a thanksgiving for Rasputin's death. Rasputin, invited to supper at the residence of Prince Youssoupov, went there flanked by the prefect of police whom the prince ejected. Then he was killed and his body, thrown in the Neva, from which it was fished, was buried in the crypt beneath the chapel at Tsarskoie Selo. After the fall of the empire, the body was exhumed, spat on, destroyed.

Sic semper, perhaps. A blackmailing tyrant in Germany's pay, Rasputin was hated as thoroughly as Nikolai was despised. Other sovereigns had been feared, loathed, revered, ignored and forgot. For Nikolai Alexandrovitch there was only contempt, in which his wife joined. She regarded him as Catherine the Greater regarded Peter the Small and, through a myopia which the glare of regalia may have induced, regarded herself as another Star of the North.

An ungracious woman, tactless, acrimonious

and stupid, a woman who never unbent and never smiled, she was highly imaginative. Marie of Rumania, a kinswoman who was as close to her as anyone could get, said that she believed herself infallible, supreme, unique, lifted immeasurably above all mankind. It was a belief that some of the Cæsars entertained and from which their madness resulted. In sharing it, this woman may have become insane, though quite as readily her dementia—if demented she were—may have been congenital. Insanity is hereditary in the Hessian house of Brabant. Her brother's favourite recreation was tatting. But the woman's opinion of herself was otherwise and quite as agreeably exemplified. Fancying herself supernormal, she believed in spiritist mysticism, believed too that her station required that she should appear in gala robes at breakfast. The robes themselves were those of a parvenu. Yet always perhaps a false conception of religion is inseparable from bad taste in dress, and her taste was such that even after the gala vulgarity was abandoned, the smart women of Petersburg took her costumes as models of what was not to be worn. Later still, she affected a simplicity of attire that would have been ostentatious were it not for the ribbons of jewels that she wore even in the privacy of her own apartments, where she sat by the hour, without moving, without speaking, lost in some dream, perhaps of Orlov, who had killed himself and whose grave she covered with flowers and tears.

It was years later that the mujik appeared and departed. Yet when this woman also departed, and on a journey that took her farther and deeper than any empress ever went, the guards at Tsarskoie Selo shouted their derision:

"Goodbye, Madame Rasputin!"

Her husband has been described as a shadow. A shadow, yes, but a shadow that crushed. Long before, on what is known as Bloody Sunday, a body of workmen set out to present a petition to him, their little father. Before they could reach the Winter Palace, their little father had them mowed. A few, that were wounded merely, survived. It was forbidden to collect a kopeck for them.

At that time the orgy had been resumed. Yet for the fair chalices of crime, the jewelled cups of mud and blood, and that table set with the épergnes of felony, the tuberoses of torture and imperial behests, another reveller, a noceur gayer than all the autocrats of all the Russias, stood by, laughing and jesting, waiting with gallant unconcern until the clock should strike.

When the clock did strike, when Nikolai Alexandrovitch after being deported was shot, the alien and perhaps unconsidered verdict was that he had been murdered. On another plane that ruling may have been reversed. Long since, a court of last resort may have decided that the rifle that killed him was charged only—and yet how amply!—with the tears, the groans, the cries of the helpless, sent to typhus, to insanity, to death, massacred at his command.

Commonsense might have preserved him. But in his case, in view of the indigent mentality of his presumptive ancestors, commonsense would have been abnormal. Instead was a derangement, clinically known as uranomania. A dwarf fancied himself divine. It was a family illusion which, other things being equal, he might have retained. His wife interfered. She also had illusions. She fancied that she looked like Marie Antoinette. It was Bazaine whom she resembled. Anything is possible. The day may come when she will be canonised.

In Hungary, Attila is a saint. In Russia, Alix of Hesse may be beatified. Even otherwise, when history is more intelligently viewed, it may be realised that the powers unseen guided this woman to open the prison in which Ivan caged a nation and for that, it may be, men will rise and call her blessed.

Previously, during a revolution that succeeded the Japanese war, this woman and that shadow hid in a palace that even from afar one was forbidden to stop and look at. Guarded by sotnias of Cossacks, there they crouched. Not alone. Terror crouched there also. Through grated casements the kramola peered. From that mysterious tribunal of the revolutionists, fluttered the death-heads that the previous incumbent knew and from which he, too, had shrunk.

In proportion as graves multiplied and the population of Siberia increased, the revolution waned. With a rictus, Terror passed, waving a hand, calling, "Au plaisir!" When he returned, he came riding a whirlwind that startled a world already inured to the startling and in which the seven times twisted coil of state snapped like a withered twig.

The cell, the knout, torture, exile, insanity, death, what could be more instructive? For centuries Russia had had a university training in all that was meant and done by the tsar's command. There is no shape of demonism, no form of horror that she did not know by heart. That poor heart of hers was a doctor of philosophy in imperial crime. When, therefore, the tsar ceased to instruct and it was Russia that taught, the benefits of her liberal education leaped.

Hunland, long since, had launched her holy crusade. Russia, then, was needy as a knife-grinder. Internally disorganised, bureaucratically corrupt, she lacked every equipment, brains included. Otherwise she was admirably prepared. There were Huns in the army, in the navy, in the ministry of war, at the tsar's elbow, in his bed. It was from these batrachian influences that bolshevism afterward developed. Germany paralysed Russia with that ankylosis which was to make her wolfishly hideous and rid her of religion, commerce, money and sense. But the situation, highly problematic, has another aspect which, shortly, will be considered. Meanwhile, gangrened already, Russia fought.

Presently the Wilhelmstrasse, confronted by collapse, floated offers of ambiguous peace. The allies rejected them. Privately the Kaiser applied to his kinswoman, Alix of Hesse, granddaughter of Victoria, of whom he was grandson. In the service of a cousin and of Germany, the Russian empress ordered a masquerade. The mask was famine. Russia beheld that spectre, conjured, a jack-in-the-box, by a woman. There was food in plenty, only it was hidden. The famine was bogus, hence the disguise.

The Duma lifted it. Behind, was the tsaritsa. Behind her were the court reactionaries. Behind them was the prefect of police. All were evoking the spectre, inciting riots, serving Germany, engineering a separate peace.

The Duma informed the tsar. For reply, the tsar ukased the Duma out. The Duma ignored the ukase. Ignored it! Any former tsar would have had every canaille in the assembly first knouted, then dispatched. But formerly there were two Russias; one above, the other below; one, the tsar; the other, the nation. With a sleight-of-hand unparalleled and incomparable, the Duma transposed them.

Nikolai Alexandrovitch was then at military headquarters. He started for Petrograd. On the train he was the autocrat from whom everything emanated, emperor of All the Russias, viceroy of the Divine, sovereign of a hundred races, lord of myriad hosts, an anthropomorphic god. When he alighted, he was the perception of a perceiver, a bundle of nothing who ceased shortly to be even that.

"Omnia fui, nihil prodest," said an expiring Cæsar, whom this final Cæsar might have mim-

micked. Might have, yes. He lacked the wit.

Over Russia, then, night still hung. Beyond was a dawn that was to send that night reeling back into the enigma of history from which Russia had come. The night was basaltic. The dawn was livid. In search of one like it, astronomers will have to look in the astral. It was the dawn of primitive man. From the night of an ended orgy, Russia, livid as that dawn, lapsed back to the stone age.

History has no parallel for the relapse. But the benefits of a very liberal education had made Russia a saint and a savage, a millionaire in rags, a genius without culture, an entity to whom meum and tuum were transposable abstractions, and which produced a type that fused idealism and knavery, the spiritual and the brute, superstition and intelligence, a type that craving anarchy endured absolutism and which resulted in what the world had never seen, a nation attacked by hydrophobia.

Hydrophobia is excessive, yet, when a shadow alighted from a train, a page of history turned, the great book of autocracy closed, and with a crash so loud that the noise shook down a prison's walls. A hundred and eighty million ignorant, helpless, hungry, angry, innocent prisoners found that they were free.

Dumbly, as prisoners will, they had dreamed of freedom. Impotently, as prisoners do, they had struggled for it. But in the dream, they had no belief; in the struggle, no conviction. It was all too utopian. When, suddenly, overnight, without conscious effort, Utopia stretched before them, it set them mad. What had seemed utopian became bedlam.

Madmen have a point of view which, when considered, is always interesting. The idea of these insane children, of some of them at least, was to destroy everything, destroy the world, build it anew. The idea seems insane, but seen from an angle higher than our own, may not the world need refurbishing? In occult sanctuaries where causes appear and criticism vanishes, sovietism is viewed as a supernormal phenomenon, propelled from planes where events are marshalled, and designed to be the obstetricy of universal palingenesis. If the view is correct nothing can prevail against it. But it may not be correct. In convulsive accouchements Greece tried to save her soul and lost her independence. Similarly, Rome dissolved from a republic into an empire and France saw the royal lilies change into imperial bees. Scepticism is history's bedfellow. History doubts that Russia's travail will be less abortive, though philosophy believes that it may be a boon. For assuming that bolshevism proceeds from a supermundane impulsion, the design may be to provide the world in general and communism in particular with an object lesson in the slavery and rationed misery that constitute the triumph of soviet ideals. Unfortunately, an age of enlightenment has never dawned for the proletariat and from philosophy clairvoyance has been withheld.

Yet when Germany launched her holy crusade, a chela admonished:—"Watch Russia! Great things will come from there."

What are these things? The Lords of Karma alone can tell. But Muhammad is suggestive. The Prophet said that paradise lies in the shadow of swords. Muhammad was pleasantly figurative and so are the swords. But, to reach paradise, always there is a desert to cross, a desert swept by simooms, peopled with djinns. The Lords of Karma alone can tell what simooms await humanity.

New York, June, 1920.

H
3
1925

perleggi